A JOURNEY OF A JAYHAWKER

W. Y. Morgan

© 2025, W. Y. Morgan (domaine public)
Édition : BoD · Books on Demand, 31 avenue Saint-Rémy, 57600 Forbach, bod@bod.fr
Impression : Libri Plureos GmbH, Friedensallee 273, 22763 Hamburg (Allemagne)
ISBN : 978-2-3225-9486-3
Dépôt légal : Avril 2025

Table of Contents

A JOURNEY OF A JAYHAWKER

W. Y. Morgan

A JOURNEY OF A JAYHAWKER

BY W. Y. MORGAN

PREFACE.

A JOURNEY OF A JAYHAWKER.

IRELAND.

FRANCE.

ITALY.

SWITZERLAND.

GERMANY.

HOLLAND AND BELGIUM.

ENGLAND.

A JOURNEY OF A JAYHAWKER

BY
W. Y. MORGAN

WITH ILLUSTRATIONS BY
ALBERT T. REID

MONOTYPED AND PRINTED BY
CRANE & COMPANY, PRINTERS
TOPEKA
1905

Copyright 1905,
By W. Y. MORGAN.

PREFACE.

These letters were written to the Hutchinson Daily News, and are printed in book form without revision. With this understanding the reader will kindly overlook inconsistencies and inaccuracies, which easily creep into what is only an impression and not a study. Any other mistakes are to be charged to the printer and proof-reader, who are likewise to be credited for the correct grammar and English which may be found in some places.

There is no excuse for the publication of these letters. No one is guilty except the writer, and he is responsible only to his conscience, which is not sensitive.

W. Y. MORGAN.

HUTCHINSON, KANSAS, December 1, 1905.

To the
PEOPLE OF HUTCHINSON,
Who have stood for much from the same
source, and for whom there is no
relief in sight, this book is
respectfully dedicated.

A JOURNEY OF A JAYHAWKER.

GOING TO EUROPE.

BOSTON, May 25, 1905.

When one decides to make a European trip he immediately becomes impressed with the importance of his intention, and thinks that everyone else is likewise affected. Of course this is a mistake, but you have to stop and think before you realize it. You go down the street imagining everyone is saying, "There is a man who is going to Europe." In fact, the other fellow is probably merely wondering whether or not you will pay the two dollars you owe him or stand him off for another thirty days. You are in an exhilarated state. You think over the cherished desires of a lifetime to see London, Paris, Rome, and the places made famous by history. You can't pick up a paper but you read some reference to a place or thing which you are going to see across the Atlantic, and which ordinarily you would skip as you do a patent-medicine advertisement. You go to reading the accounts of Emperor William's plans as if you would soon meet William and talk them over with him. You read about the comings and goings of nobility and wonder if the pope knows you are likely to call on him some day in July, and whether the Swiss Guards will realize the honor of a visit from an American citizen by the name of Morgan or Jones. You read of European travel and sights, and, worst of all, you actually get to believe the things. In fact, you work yourself up to a fine point of enthusiasm and in your mind go cavorting around among ancient heroes and crowned heads. As a first guess I would say that probably the most successful part of a trip to the Old World is the one you take in advance.

As soon as I disclosed my European intentions, I began to get advice from friends and old travelers. This is a trying experience. Everybody has ideas as to what should be done, and no two will agree. One of the first questions to be settled is that of clothing. The importance of this is impressed upon the prospective tourist. In the first place I am told to take no baggage except the very simplest that can be carried in the hand. In the second place I am advised that when traveling in Europe, even more than in this country, one should be prepared for all kinds of climate and be ready with the proper clothes to meet every emergency. Every bit of information is absolutely as true as common law or the gospel, for the informant has either made the trip, or his wife's cousin has, or he knows a man who knows another man who did,—and you are told what happened with all the harrowing details. Clothes do not make the man or the woman, but they help out a lot. So that our friends will realize the difficulties we may meet. I will admit that we are going to the "simple" extreme, taking only light baggage, very little more than a clean collar and a pleasant smile. If royalty wants to call upon us, royalty will not find us prepared with the clothes required by the books of etiquette, unless I can hire a dress suit or borrow one from the head waiter.

I have also discovered that it is going to be difficult to please everybody with our route. Nearly every person has something that just must be seen, and not to do so would make a trip to Europe a flat failure. Most of these important places are dug up by inspiration from the memory of some novel or play. There is the scientific man who urges German universities, the musically inclined who would make Wagnerian objects the great points, the historical student who prescribes battlefields, the sportive gent who urges Monte Carlo, the classical enthusiast who can think of nothing less than a thousand years old, the art-lover who has a list of seventy-seven different styles of Madonnas, the novel-reader who would wander over the country of Scott, the social oracle who would spend the time in London and "Paree," the enthusiast in civics who is interested in government railroads, the initiative and referendum of Switzerland, and the man whose ideas of a trip abroad are condensed in the parting injunction, "Take one for me at Munich or Heidelberg." It is shocking to see the disappointed look of the friendly adviser if you do not agree with him that his recommendation is the great thing in Europe. A friend of mine who is an archæologist said: "Of course you are going to Greece?" Now I had not thought of Greece, and ventured to say so. "What, not going to Greece!" was the withering answer in a tone which plainly meant that you were undoubtedly going to throw your opportunity away like an empty sack when the peanuts are gone. Another type of adviser is the man who says: "You must see the Coliseum," when you know the man would not know the Coliseum if he were to meet it in the road. He has simply heard some one say something about the Coliseum, and takes that word in order to show off his superior knowledge of the sights of Europe. During the weeks of preparation we have made "itineraries" to suit the suggestions of our friends. It is easy to make an itinerary, and no trouble at all to change it the next day when a more profitable route is offered. On a rough estimate I should say that in the last few weeks we have made European itineraries enough to take about seventeen years' time, and we are intending to be away only about three months. The fact is that while Europe is only a little continent, not near as big as the United States, it has been fought over, scrapped over, built over, written about and has been doing business for so many hundreds of years that there is hardly a pin-point on the map which for some good reason you do not want to visit. It is like taking a newspaper article about seven columns long and condensing it to a small paragraph. You feel you are cutting out all the really good places, and about the extent of your trip is to the points to which you have ordered your mail sent and where you have to go to change trains.

And then there is the friend who can't go to Europe and who could hardly get to Newton if he had to pay for a round-trip ticket, who comfortingly says: "I wouldn't go to Europe until I had seen all of my own country." This remark has been made to me so often in the last few weeks that I have learned to dodge when I see it coming. I have traveled around some in the United States, and as a matter of fact the people in one section are pretty much the same as the people in another, and it is people that I like to see and not mountains or museums. Of course some parts are more so than others. There is no State like Kansas and no people like Kansans. The object of a trip to Europe is to see something different, as different as possible. It is to get the local "color" for the things you read about. It is to learn if the men and women of the Old World are as they are pictured in books, and to compare them with the people whom you associate with every day at home. I am told that in Paris even little children can talk French, and that in Germany the people stand it to have an emperor and never organize any boss-buster movements or bolt the party nominations. I have read about these things all my life, and they may be true. I want to see them. I am not from Missouri, but I have lived near enough to want to be shown.

We sailed from Hutchinson on the Santa Fe. After touching at a few places we reached Boston safely, and unless the police intervene we will embark this afternoon on the White Star steamship Arabic. It is still two hours until we go aboard but I am already seasick, or am imagining how it will feel, which is nearly as bad. I am not afraid of water. I have lived too long on the Arkansas and Cow creek and my boyhood was spent on the shores of the Cottonwood. But nevertheless and notwithstanding, I feel as I think everybody must when he takes his first long ocean voyage. I never noticed so many accounts of wrecks as I have in the last month. If there was an item in a newspaper about the wreck of some ocean steamer or the drowning of a passenger, and I did not see the piece, some friend always did, and brought it to me to comfort me. Statistics prove that it is as safe to travel across the ocean in a steamship as across Kansas in a railroad train. This is comforting, but statistics do not look big and substantial when you contemplate a week's existence with nothing but a few boards and bolts between yourself and the place where McGinty went. One little man in a little old boat seems mighty small in the middle of a big ocean.

LEAVING THE LAND.

Steamship Arabic, May 29, 1905.

In spite of the fact that a trip across the Atlantic is not considered dangerous or exceptional, there is always a lot of sentiment which comes up into the throat of the traveler when he goes aboard the ship that is to take him out of his own country and across the ocean to a foreign land. Long before the Arabic was to sail it was filled with passengers and friends who had come to say good-by and wave farewell. The custom is whenever a friend is to start on such a trip to accompany him or her to the dock, send flowers to be placed in the stateroom, and to stand on the wharf and wave a handkerchief until the responding figure on the deck of the ship is no longer recognizable in the distance. Of course, we were so far from home that there was nobody to do these honors for wandering Kansans, so we picked out a few nice-looking people who seemed to be there for curiosity and vigorously shouted and waved good-by to them, and they had the good taste to respond. A Colorado man who had been on the trip before told me afterward that the young fellow who had called so cheerily and waved so vigorously at him as the steamer pulled away from land, was a hotel porter whom he had hired for a half-dollar to come to the wharf and bid him godspeed on his journey.

The Arabic turned away from the dock at 4.30 in the afternoon of May 25, and steamed slowly and majestically down the harbor and out toward the ocean with a half-dozen little pilot-boats and revenue cutters whistling and dancing like a lot of little dogs frisking and playing around a big dog as it walks down the street. The old ship Constitution, heroine of America's early naval warfare, was passed, the forts and the navy yard with the modern warships and guns, the last island and the last American flag faded into the distance, and a solemn thought of leaving one's native land and of possible seasickness makes one choke with patriotism and foreboding. It is too late now to back out. There is no chance to get off. For a week the ship will never stop, and there will be no place upon which the eye can rest except water and sky. A flood of sentiment rushes through one and leaks a little at the eyes as the mind turns to those who have been so near and dear and are now to be so far away. That is the feeling experienced by all travelers, and I want to be recorded present and voting on the question, although as a matter of fact while the Arabic was leaving the dock and country I was quarreling with the purser over the stateroom and trying to get the steward to help me handle baggage when he was so full of American liquor that he could do nothing but say "yessir" (hic) and smile.

NO TIME FOR SENTIMENT.

No doubt everyone has noticed how the apparently little things of life occupy us at most critical and important times. I remember when at a certain stage I was accomplishing an object to which I had worked industriously and whole-heartedly. I should have been filled with happiness and pride as I faced a large crowd of people. As a matter of fact I was miserable because my collar did not fit my shirt and kept bobbing up and down in a refractory way. The first time I saw Niagara Falls, whither I had gone to be overcome with the grandeur and beauty of the scene, I put in all my time trying to find a place to get a sandwich. It is said that when Gladstone was making his great fight for Irish home rule he was sitting on his bench in parliament, apparently wrapped in deep thought. His colleagues did not disturb him, for they supposed he was pondering the question which was agitating every mind. Finally he straightened himself up and said to himself, but so those near could hear: "After all, I will plant that rosebush in the front instead of at the side of the doorway." The energetic man who is traveling amid picturesque and historical places puts in more time figuring out time-tables and wondering whether he will get dinner in a dining-car or at a lunch station, than he does in soulful meditation on the wonders of nature or the handiwork of man. And the general run of women, I am firmly convinced by circumstantial evidence, will approach the subject of a European trip or a church wedding, not with the thoughts of the lands to be visited or the responsibility to be assumed, but with minds full of the problem of whether four shirtwaists and a skirt will do better than two dresses. This peculiarity of humanity has often impressed me, so I was not surprised when I realized as I returned more or less triumphant from my battles with purser and steward that I missed most of the thrills and throbs that had been promised me by all the guidebooks and books of travel that I had read.

An ocean voyage is being robbed of most of its terrors. The Arabic is a big ship, one of the largest. It stretches out over so many waves that it does very little rolling or plunging. We have been out for three days and there have been really no cases of seasickness. I fully expected to be seasick, and it is a great disappointment. However, I am not going to ask the company to refund my fare on that account. Everybody is afraid of seasickness, and down in his heart everybody wishes that everybody else might be sick and he alone left to proudly walk the deck and smile at the victims. The only person who suffers from seasickness is the individual affected. You may run a sliver in your finger and the family will gather around with words of sympathy. You may get a cinder in your eye and your friends will hurry forward to help get it out. But if you are suffering with seasickness, and death would almost be welcome, your friends will only grin and their words of condolence are false and mocking.

A modern steamship is constructed for safety, comfort, and almost luxury. When you get those three qualities there is very little left of the poetry or novelty of ocean traveling. We still speak of the ship "sailing," although, of course, it doesn't. The modern ship steams. We have read all of our lives about the beautiful white-wings and the jolly jack tars. The reality is a mammoth engine out of sight, a big smoke-stack, and a lot of black, dust-covered, sweaty firemen. The "sailors" no longer climb the rigging and the masts, but go down in the hole and shovel coal. My ideas of the sea came from Oliver Optic. I want to hear the boatswain pipe, the mate's command, "All hands belay ship," and see the captain as he stands at his post and with an occasional "Steady, my hearties," direct the seamen as they sing their songs and clamber up the masts. That is beauty and poetry. But the reality is that the captain whistles down the tube to the engineer and he gives the order, "More coal, you sons of guns; stop that noise and fire up." That is fact, and makes traveling comfortable but not soul-inspiring.

The White Star line, on which we are traveling, belongs to the big steamship company merger, formed by Pierpont Morgan a few years ago. It is really owned by American capital and controlled by American financiers, but the ships carry the British flag and are manned by British officers and men. England manages things so that it pays to carry the English flag. I have a great deal of respect for England. With all our American enterprise, energy and ability, we look like a tallow candle beside an electric light when it comes to ships and international commerce. The government of England always looks after its shipping interests and encourages capital to send English vessels and English crews carrying English merchandise to the furthermost parts. Prizes, bounties, subsidies and favors of all kinds have been used to make the merchant marine of Great Britain greater than that of the rest of the world. The English are a great people, and they are conscious of it. And they see to it that everybody else understands the fact. There isn't anything in this American-owned ship that comes from the United States except what the passengers have in their baggage. The crew from captain to cook are English. The supplies are all bought in England. The ships are built and repaired at Belfast. Coal for the voyage both ways comes from Wales. English meats and even ice-cream are purchased in Liverpool for the round trip. You can't buy an American postage stamp, and United States money is not taken except at exchange below par. The American who has been going through life under the impression that America is the whole thing has his feelings stepped on nearly every time he turns around.

The daily life on a steamship is a good deal like I am told it is on a limited Santa Fe Pullman train, only there is a little more room. There are all kinds of people on the Arabic, mostly from England, the United States or Boston. Soon after we left port I met a fellow who looked like somebody from home. I asked him where he was from, and he said Nevada. I said I was from Kansas, and he enthusiastically grasped my hand and said, "Then we are neighbors." You do get a good deal of that feeling. Afterward we met some folks from Colorado, and to see us warm up to each other would have made you think we were a long separated but happily reunited family. When anyone asks me where I hail from and I say "Kansas," the answer is nearly always "Oh." And then I shut my eyes and wait for the next remark. It never fails to come: "Do you know Carrie Nation?" If I get a fair show I generally manage in the course of conversation to incidentally ring in a few things about Kansas that they never heard before (and once in a long while something I never heard before myself). I don't have to confine myself to things I can prove. Colorado and Nevada will stand by me, and if the returning English tourists are not regretting they did not see the wonderful State of Kansas they are simply figuring me out a liar. The poet said: "How sweet it is for one's country to die." Let us add: "How sweet it is for one's country to lie."

That reminds me of a good joke on myself. An Englishman was complaining of the voyage and wishing he was in old. England. I did a little rapture talk about the ocean, and said I loved to go on the deck, watching the never-ending blue of water and sky and just lie and lie and lie there. He said: "I believe you told me you were a newspaper man."

CROSSING THE ATLANTIC.

STEAMSHIP ARABIC, June 1, 1905.

I have come to a realization of the work of Christopher Columbus. It took nerve to keep on sailing day in and day out, week in and week out, with no sight of anything that looked like land,—nothing but a great stretch of water, not even a stick in it. If I had been on board the Santa Maria I would surely have joined the crowd of sailors who wanted to quit and go home. We have come now nearly 3,000 miles through the Atlantic, and if someone had not been over the route before and we did not believe that land would appear at a certain time it would certainly look as if the ocean would never end. If Columbus were to make the trip now on the Arabic he would probably be as surprised as were the Indians when the Spaniards landed on San Salvador something over 400 years ago. The monotony of the ocean is only broken by an occasional passing ship, and a high-strung imagination. We have met or passed five ships in seven days. Each one has provided us with excitement for half a day. We took sides as to whether the strange vessel was a Cunarder, an American liner, a North German Lloyd or what not. Every line that crosses the ocean would have partisans and each corner of the argument would be vigorously sustained by expert evidence. I decided on a system. I always maintained that the ship was an American liner. By sticking to the text and not changing I hit it once, which was better than the average. Then we have long and sometimes bitter discussions as to the number of miles the Arabic will make in the next twenty-four hours. Tips are anxiously obtained from officers, sailors, stewards and cooks. Every man who ever bet in his life and some who never do at home, back their opinions with their money. And when we are not arguing or betting we are eating. Passengers on this line are full-fed. The day begins with 8 o'clock breakfast, at 10:30 a lunch is served, on deck, at 1 o'clock an elaborate lunch, at 4 o'clock tea, cakes and sandwiches are distributed, and at 7 o'clock a course dinner. People do all of these and eat sandwiches and stuff between times and then wonder why their stomachs are "disturbed."

It takes all kinds of people to make up the world, and there are samples of most of the varieties on an ocean steamer. Some of our passengers are very swell and some are very bum. But they meet on the level—provided you can call the deck of a ship level when it is usually tilted one way or the other at an angle of 20 to 30 degrees. In the spirit of investigation I listened to the talk of a couple of ladies who are society leaders and members of the 400 at home. The subjects they discussed were babies, servants and clothes, and they talked just about like the women-folks of Kansas. There is a touch of human nature through all of us.

When I left home I decided not to change my watch until I got to Europe. At Boston I was only one hour behind and could easily remember and count on that. But every day on the ocean the clock has been shoved up thirty-five minutes for the 400 miles traveled eastward the preceding twenty-four hours. When it got so we were eating noonday lunch at 8 A. M. by my watch I gave it up and turned the hands around. When we reach London we will be about six hours ahead of Hutchinson time, and anyone can see the ridiculous side of getting up at 2 o'clock in the morning and going to bed at 4 in the afternoon. By a strange coincidence the sun has changed its time for rising and setting to agree with the ship's clock.

There is great system on a big ship. Everything is done just so and no other way. I have had a hard time locating the "stewards." I never realized what a steward was before. We have a bedroom steward, who looks after the stateroom, a bath steward who runs the bathroom, a deck steward in charge of the deck, an assistant deck steward, a library steward, a smoking-room steward, a table steward, and a few more whose titles I can't remember. One steward never gets on another's line of duty. If you want a deck chair you must see the deck steward, if you want a blanket you must see the saloon steward, and so on. If I fall overboard I hope the proper steward will be around, for the system is so fine that I fear the other stewards would refuse to act until the proper steward could be called. Each steward will be expecting a tip when the voyage is ended, and if he weren't a "steward," he probably could not get it so easily.

Sunday we had religious service in the saloon. (Not the kind of a saloon that Mrs. Nation holds service in.) It was the Church of England service, but out of respect to the American passengers the reader ran in President Roosevelt's name in the prayer for the royal family. It was a quiet, beautiful day and the amount of the collection was small. I was told by an officer that when Sunday is a stormy day and the boat acts as if it might tip over most any time, the passengers contribute much more liberally to the offering than they do when the day is fair. Some people go to church on board ship who never see the inside of a church on land. I suppose they learn from the sailors the advantage of casting an anchor out to the windward.

We will see land in a few hours, the southwest coast of Ireland. A few hours later we will land at Queenstown. It will be mighty good to get one's feet on ground that doesn't move just when you don't expect it to. We will find out what has happened in the world, for we haven't had any news for a week. They are betting on whether or not the Jap and Russian fleets have met during our absence from the earth. Like a great many good things, the best part of an ocean voyage is the end. I have enjoyed the trip very much, but if I get a chance to walk back to America I will be mighty glad to take it.

IRELAND.

FIRST DAY IN IRELAND.

Cork, Ireland, June 3.

The first vivid impression made upon me in Ireland was the morning after we landed. We had come ashore late at night at Queenstown, and except for the Irish names and Irish brogue there was nothing to indicate but that we were going through an American custom-house into an American hotel. But when we went to breakfast up came the waiter attired in full dress and extra long-tailed coat with a red vest. I had always supposed the pictures of an English or Irish waiter in such livery at breakfast was a joke. It is not a joke. It is a most serious and proper attire, and I suppose an Irish waiter in a first-class hotel would as soon appear to serve breakfast without any pants as without the long swallowtail coat. And when I saw that, I knew I was far away from home.

A European breakfast is "rolls and coffee." In anticipation I had thought of hot rolls and delicious coffee. Put this down: There are no hot rolls in Ireland, and I am guessing there will be none in Europe. "Rolls" means plain, very plain, cold bread, hard and a trifle stale. The coffee is bum and the cream is skim-milk. An English hotel, for that is what Irish first-class hotels are, ought to put more into the eating and less into the waiter's uniform. Along with other Americans at that first breakfast, we joined in a howl and managed to get some eggs.

Queenstown is one of the largest and best of the British harbors. It has an important navy yard and several English warships are anchored among the numerous merchant vessels. The town is on the side of a high hill which comes down to the water's edge, and the narrow streets go up and down the slope at every angle except a right angle to the street along the waterfront. The chief resources of Queenstown are sailors and tourists, and the main occupations of the leading inhabitants are lodging-houses and saloons. Over nearly every store is the sign, "Licensed to sell ale, porter and spirits seven days in the week."

THE IRISH JAUNTING (JOLTING) CAR.

There is nothing much to Queenstown except the quaintness that comes from age and dirt, and I have seen enough American towns with the same characteristics to make this an old story. But we walked and climbed to the top of the hill, and there I saw a panorama spread out before me which will stick to my memory a good long while. The large harbor, locked on three sides and part of the fourth with land, made a blue setting for the white of the numerous ships. Little sailboats drifted over the quiet water and tugs and launches darted in and out among the big vessels. Eight-oared boats from the warships, manned with uniformed sailors from the royal navy, skimmed back and forth, the eight oars rising and falling as one. Flags were flying from mastheads, and the decks were lively with the work of the day. Up from the shore on every side except where the ocean's blue appeared, rose the greenest green hills you ever saw, and they reached to the bluest blue sky you ever saw, a frame for the picture which no artist could ever hope to portray.

An Irish woman whose son had gone to America and sent back for the mother and little sister, had never been far from home before. Leading the little girl by the hand she was walking to Queenstown and came in sight of the harbor from the top of the hill. The beauty of the scene impressed her, but she added a lesson for the benefit of the daughter: "Look at the beautiful sight and see how wonderful is the work of Nature. See the big ships side by side, and all around them their little ones."

Queenstown is the harbor for Cork, which is twelve miles up the river Lee. It is the commercial metropolis of southern Ireland and has furnished more policemen to America than any town of twice its size in the United States. Of course the first thing we did was to ride in a jaunting-car and go to Blarney Castle. The castle looks just about as it did last summer on the Pike at St. Louis. But the surrounding grounds are as pretty as they can be. I hesitate when it comes to describing the park with its stately trees, its beautiful grassy slopes crowned with wild flowers, its moss and ivy which cling to wall and tree, covering defects, revealing charms, enhancing beauties. The castle itself was built by McCarthy, king of Munster, in 1446, and while of course uninhabited and in partial ruin, is in good preservation, to make an Irish bull of it. We climbed to the top, we reveled in the rich scene around us, kissed the blarney stone and cheerfully gave the care-taker twice the usual fee because she said Americans were the best people on earth. Then we had the nicest lunch that has come our way since we left Kansas—an Irish lunch of bread and butter, cold ham and milk. We had traveled all morning and climbed among ruins from 12 to 2 o'clock. If you want the best lunch on earth, no matter what it is made of, climb towers for a couple of hours.

There are some things that are peculiarly Irish. The jaunting-car is one of them. It is the favorite vehicle for driving. It looks like a two-wheel cart, driver's seat in the front end and passengers' seats back to back, facing outward. My fellow-traveler, Mr. McGregor, says the Irish brogue has perverted into jaunting-car the real name, which is jolting-car. The driver is always a good fellow and he keeps the horse on the gallop much of the time. You have to learn to keep your seat on a jaunting-car as you do on a bicycle. You also have to learn to weigh the statements of your driver as to distances and legends as you do the promises of a candidate for office. We suggested to one that a jaunting-car driver had to lie. "We never lie, sir," said the Irishman. "But we stretch it a little."

After a week on shipboard, during which time I had patiently shaved myself, I yearned for the comforting work of a good barber. At the best hotel in Cork, a city of 80,000 people, I went to the best barber shop in town. The chair was just like a common wooden kitchen chair, only not quite so comfortable. There was a head-rest made out of a two-by-four scantling, and when the barber pulled my head back onto that I knew my dream of a comfortable shave was to be a nightmare. He made the lather in a wash-basin and I think he honed the razor on a grindstone. It cut all right when it didn't pull out by the roots. When the operation was finished he combed my hair with my head still back, washed my face with cold water and rubbed it with a coarse towel. The barber charged me twopence (equivalent to four cents). And that was my first experience with a European tonsorial artist. Perhaps sometime in my life I have felt cross at a barber at home because the razor pulled or because he squirted bay rum into my eye. But in the future I will never murmur, except to recall my experience in Cork and thank God for American barbers.

The day we came to Cork there was an election for poor-law guardians, only a local affair, but I attended. The voting is by Australian ballot just as in America. The suffrage is restricted to householders, including those who pay a certain rent, and women vote the same as men. The politicians at the polling-place treated me well and explained all the methods. One of the workers told the judge that they should let me vote, as when he had visited his brother in America they had let him vote twice while there. I proposed that if they would let me vote for poor-law guardians in the county of Cork I would let any of them vote for councilman in the Fourth ward of Hutchinson. We had a good friendly visit, and it was easy to see that Irishmen are politicians in the Old World as well as the New. After a man or woman voted he or she was always given a drink at the nearest place where "spirits" are sold. But when the polls closed instead of going ahead and counting the votes, the judges adjourned until noon the next day—the invariable custom. It was not until the afternoon following the election when it was learned who "stood at the top of the poll." We couldn't stand the pressure that long in America.

There were placards up all around telling the voters to "vote the straight ticket," "vote for the interest of labor," and "vote for your own interests." The newspapers the next day told of the vicious conduct of the opposition and the immoral practices resorted to. But as a rule the Irish people are like Americans, accepting the result with good feeling and promises of what will be done to the other fellows the next time.

BY KILLARNEY'S LAKES.

Killarney, June 8, 1905.

We have spent four days in the Irish mountains and have ridden a hundred miles in a jaunting-car and coach. I have had mountain scenery, lake scenery and plain scenery for every meal in the day. I enjoy scenery, but I fear I am getting it in too large quantities and am having it shaken too well while taking. Sunday was spent in Glengariff, a picturesque place where the mountains rise abruptly from the salt water of Bantry bay. Monday we coached from Glengariff to Killarney and Tuesday we did the lakes with a jaunting-car, slightly assisted by a row-boat. The Irish mountains are not as high as the Rocky Mountains, but they are a very good imitation. The Rockies are grand and beautiful. The mountains of Cork and Kerry are pretty and beautiful. The Irish mountains are covered with green. It is as if the Rocky Mountains were smaller, covered with ivy and moss, dotted here and there with whitewashed cottages and flocks of sheep, and topped with a blue sky which is bluer than any indigo and clearer than any crystal.

There are several ruined castles about Killarney. I am already getting to shy at ruined castles. The proposal to visit one makes my feet ache as an approaching thunder-storm affects some people's corns. We first went to Muckross Abbey, a well-preserved ruin about 400 years old. The Muckross family, which owned the estate, has played out, and the property has been bought by Guinness, the Dublin brewer, who was made a lord by Queen Victoria. Whatever the earl of Kenmare does not own around Killarney belongs to Guinness. You can imagine how Muckross Abbey looked 300 years ago when the old monks lived there and occupied the cells and cloister now unroofed. The banquet hall has a big fireplace and there are dark spiral stairways running up and down such as you read about in Ivanhoe. On the tombstones are inscriptions telling of the virtues and sanctity of knights and lords who would be considered tough bats if they lived nowadays and swaggered around as they did in the good old times. I like to look at old tombstones and wonder what the men who lie beneath them would say if they could read the catalogue of virtues accredited to them. I always think of the little girl who had evidently been visiting Muckross Abbey, or some such place, and anxiously inquired if the people in those days did not bury bad folks, as all who were interred there were supremely good. And then the thought comes up that all of these men were great and strong in their time, making history and imagining that they were cutting a gash in the world. Now they are forgotten and their deeds unknown, and they are the subjects of sportive remarks by tourists from a country they never heard of.

The lakes of Killarney have been praised in prose and verse, and they are up to the advance advertising. They are not large, but they nestle among the mountains and reflect on their clear surface the heights that surround them. There is a legend everywhere and the Irish driver knows them all. Here is a reasonable one: One of the O'Donohues, which family was once the royal power in Kerry, was hunting in the mountains. He met the devil, and the two had an altercation in which O'Donohue got decidedly the best of the argument. The devil became so angry that he bit a big chunk out of a mountain. O'Donohue took his shillelah and hit the devil so hard a crack that he dropped the mouthful of mountain into the lake. This tale must be true, for as the driver said: "There's the place the devil bit and it is called so to this day, and out in the lake is the little island of rock, just as the devil dropped it into the water."

Everybody who has read Tom Moore—and if anyone has not he should do so—will remember the lines:

'e is not in the wide world a valley so sweet

e vale in whose bosom the bright waters meet."

The meeting of the three Killarney lakes was referred to, and Moore was telling truth as well as poetry. The upper lake and the middle lake narrow to small streams and flow together as they merge into the little rosebud of a mouth which the lower lake puts up to greet them. There is a rapid which the boat shoots for a sixpence, but it was not thrilling. In the triangular park made by lakes and mountains are said to be specimens of every kind of tree known. The driver told this proudly, but when I called for a cottonwood he couldn't produce. Then I told him all about the wonderful cottonwood, and he promised to see the keeper and find out why they couldn't have one in Killarney.

That reminds me of my experience with music. The first morning I awoke in Ireland at Queenstown I heard the voices of a number of sailors of the royal navy, and as the melodious sounds rolled into the window I was surprised to realize that they were singing "Under the Anheuser-Busch." At the hotel in Cork the orchestra played the same. At the theatre that night it was greeted with an encore. The driver on the jaunting-car whistled the tune. And last night when I had made friends with a cottager and was sitting with him by the side of a peat fire and he was telling me of Ireland's woes, his little girl came in and he proceeded to show her off. First he had her sing an old Gaelic song. Then he said, "Now give us an American song," and she responded with "Under the Anheuser-Busch."

I have hardly met an Irishman but has told me he had brothers and sisters in America. At Glengariff the hotel proprietor said at least 2,000 young men and women had gone to America from that parish in the last few years—the brightest and best of the young people, he said—nearly all of them to Boston. From Killarney nearly all go to New York. I told them how Boston and New York were ruled by the Irish, and put the question as to why the Irish couldn't run Ireland. I am trying to answer that conundrum to my own satisfaction, and am gathering ideas on the subject from everyone I meet.

The ordinary Irish village like Killarney is a quaint picture. The streets are narrow, mostly eight to twelve feet wide. The main street is about thirty feet wide. Nearly all the houses are a story or a story and a half, thatched roof, whitewashed walls, dirt floors except in one room, low ceilings, doors and windows, full of chickens, cats and children. I have not yet seen a pig in the parlor. The pig is kept in a little room at one side. But the chickens have as much liberty of the house as anybody and the goat is monarch of the outside. There is very seldom any yard, the houses being built right up to the street. The house is heated by a fireplace and the cooking is done in the same. Peat is the fuel, and it is cleaner and not sooty like coal. The dirt floor and the chickens in the house sound as though the Irish cottage would be dirty, but the whitewash and the scrubbing-brush fight on the other side, and you don't get that impression. The women-folks are always neat-looking and everybody is pleasant and cheerful. Every window has a window-box of geraniums. There are usually so many children that the house does not hold them, and the street is always filled with them. Remember when you are driving through a town the street is filled with children, and if you are an American and not used to it your heart will be jumping into your throat for fear some of them will be run over—but I am told they never are.

After the chickens and the children the most novel sight is the donkeys with their two-wheel carts, the only ordinary carriages for passengers or freight of the people. The donkey is the size of our mountain burro, and has the same degree of intelligent expression. All of the hauling is done by this patient animal, and he is looked upon as a valued member of the family.

In riding or walking the rule of the country is the same as in England—turn to the left. I have not yet gotten over the yearning to grab the lines from the driver when he turns to the left to avoid a passing carriage. Fortunately the other driver is always fool enough to also turn to the left. I confided my trouble to an Irish driver, and he said it was ridiculous to turn to the right.

One of my traveling companions is a man who chews tobacco, and he had neglected to lay in a supply before leaving America. No one else used the weed that way and there was no help for him. The Irish chew and smoke the same plug tobacco, very dry and not tasting like American tobacco. For a week my friend had been looking through shops trying to find something that would touch the spot. Last night soon after reaching Killarney he came to me greatly excited and said, "Hurry! the finest scenery since we left home." Away we went down the narrow street and up to a window in which was a familiar shape and a sign, "Battle Ax." I don't chew myself, but I have some bad habits, and I could appreciate the tear of joy that glistened in my fellow-traveler's eye as he gazed on that sign and felt that he had met an old friend just from home.

IRELAND AND THE IRISH.

DUBLIN, June 9, 1905.

In my short stay in the Emerald Isle I have endeavored to find out what is the matter with Ireland. Why is it that a country of great beauty and resources, with a healthful and productive climate, an intelligent and attractive people, is a country where poverty is widespread, although disguised by picturesque surroundings, and is accepted in such a matter-of-fact and almost nonchalant manner? Why is it that the population of Ireland is decreasing while the number of successful and prosperous Irishmen is rapidly increasing in America, Canada, and Australia? A very intelligent Irishman at Glengariff told me why it was, and this in brief is his story:

A thousand years ago Ireland was ahead of all neighbors in education, religion, and refinement. Then came the civil wars between the chieftains. Then came England, and by utilizing the demoralization of the civil wars and playing one chieftain against another, acquired sovereignty. But this was only nominal, for the Irish chieftains did not submit permanently. In Glengariff country the O'Sullivans maintained practical independence. Finally the English rulers adopted the policy of confiscating the land of the rebellious chieftains and giving it to English soldiers and queen's favorites. In many places this meant the massacre of the people. The O'Sullivans and their fighting men who escaped went to France and continued to strike at their Saxon foes. But the land passed into the ownership of strangers, who kept it only for the profit they could get out of it. The new Irish nobles lived in London and their agents ran the estates. When the nobles needed more money their agents advanced the rents. If the people who tilled the soil and whose tenancy had been unquestioned for generations, could not pay, they were evicted. Families were ejected from the places they had cultivated and made valuable and were set out on the road. This was done not without fighting for their rights by the Irish people, but by the superior force of English soldiers. No Irish farmer owns his place—he is only a tenant at the mercy of his absentee landlord, who does not know him. In other countries the feudal tenure has not worked so harshly, because the landlords lived among the people and were bound to them by ties of race, common history, and natural affection. But the fact that there was no way for an Irishman to get his own home, or have a reasonable chance to advance in fortune or freedom, sent the brightest to America, and left the others to struggle hopelessly along, knowing that the best they could do was to "pay the rent," which was fixed like some railroad charges in the United States, on the basis of "all the traffic would stand."

From the parish of Glengariff more than half the young men and at least half the young women have gone to the land of promise across the sea, and are sending back money to help the parents and brothers and sisters at home, either to "pay the rent" or to pay their passage to America.

What is true at Glengariff applies to the rest of Ireland. The ancient chieftains, the O'Sullivans, the O'Donohues, the McCartys and the rest, were succeeded by absentee landlords, and the law of supply and demand backed up by the English army simply worked out. At Killarney whatever land does not belong to the earl of Kenmare is the property of Guinness. The lakes and rivers are full of fish, but no Irishman can catch a fish; the mountains are full of game, but no one can hunt it except the owner of the estate. The farms are well tilled, but no one can buy the land upon which he works. It makes an American mad, and he says, "How do you stand it?" But it is the law, and along every country road there is a policeman and behind the policeman is the power of England. Far up on the mountain-side, several miles from town or settlement, I saw a fine stone building which on inquiry I found was a police station. The police, or the constabulary, as they are called, were not there to protect the lives of the citizens, but to prevent hunting and fishing in the brooks and mountains. So, after all, it is no wonder the Irishman leaves his beautiful island and emigrates to America.

The Irish have kept the English Parliament in an uproar for a generation on this land question, and in recent years they have secured some friendly legislation. A court can now fix the rent rate on appeal—but the English government names the court. So far as Englishmen of the present day are concerned they would be glad to get out of the Irish problem and let the Irish have their land, but of course that can't be done. The present parliament provided a plan for the eventual purchase of land by tenant, at a price to be fixed by the court if the two parties cannot agree. This is a step in the right direction and the Irish are glad of it, but as my Glengariff friend said, "It will not do any good in this generation." And the exodus to America continues.

The Irish are very intelligent. I do not think the poor people of any other country are naturally so bright and so full of perception and understanding. They are kind and gentle. They are affectionate and patriotic. The English say they are "lazy," but under the circumstances you could hardly expect them to be yearning for work, when more work means more valuable holdings, and that only means more rent for the landlord. The Irish have a reputation among the English for honesty. They are religious, and I thought at first they gave too much to the church and did not keep enough for themselves, when I saw the large and rich cathedrals. But, as an Irishman told me, "We'd rather give to the Lord than the landlord." Public schools are providing education for the rising generation, and in the public school the boys and girls are being taught the Irish language and prepared for the coming fight which the Irish must make to capture Ireland—not probably for an independent government, but for actual ownership of the Irish soil.

Taxes are heavy. The burden of taxation is the income tax. "That falls on the landlord," the thoughtless might say. Not on your life. The tax is simply added to the rent. There are fine public roads in Ireland, as good in the country districts as Main street in Hutchinson will be when it is paved. The only advantage a despotic government has over a popular government is that it builds better roads. When the people elect their own road bosses and levy their own road taxes I notice the roads are not so good as when some prince or cabinet minister who does not care what the people think, levies the tax and orders the road built right. The Irish statesmen are struggling for Irish ownership of Irish soil and an Irish parliament to deal with Irish affairs. They are "getting on," and, as I said before, they make so much trouble in the English Parliament that I know the English would be glad to get rid of Irish local politics and give them back their parliament, if it were not for pride,—and the next parliament may cut out the pride.

I want to record one fact which I was surprised to find. The Irish are very temperate. I have been in city, town and country for ten days, have not been careful about keeping in the nice parts of town, and I have seen only one man under the influence of liquor, and he was an English sailor at Queenstown. This is in spite of the fact that every inn and grocery sells "spirits" and nearly everybody seems to drink them if he or she has the price. Perhaps the reason is that in Ireland all the liquor-selling is done by women—barmaids. Perhaps the influence of women behind the bar makes for temperance. I won't state that as my conclusion, but just submit it for what it is worth to those who are trying to solve the liquor question in other countries.

Dublin is a good deal like an American city. It is full of business and not as Irish as the inland towns or Cork, although it has statues to O'Connell, Curran and Grattan, and will have one to Parnell. The lord lieutenant-governor, the representative of the king, resides at Dublin, and a big garrison of soldiers gives it an English tone.

There is a fine university, which we visited. It was started by Queen Elizabeth, and has only recently been opened to Catholics and to women. Dublin has some great stores where Irish linen and Irish lace should naturally be cheap. If Mrs. Morgan were writing this letter she could add a chapter. I will only tell this little story: I was telling an Irish driver how nice everybody had been to us in Ireland and how pleasant the Irish were to Americans. "Yis," he said. "Whin you go down the strate, everybody sez: 'There's some Americans, God bless 'em: mark up the prices on the linen and lace.'"

FRANCE.

THE CITY OF PLEASURE.

PARIS, FRANCE, June 19, 1905.

Since my last letter to The News we have been "going some," and I will leave a few ideas I may have gleaned about England until I get back there on my return from the continent. We are pushing for a short visit to Italy before the summer gets too far advanced.

To use a classical expression, Paris is a bully sort of a town. If there is anything you want and don't know where it is, I am satisfied you will find it in Paris. In England it was customary to close up and go to bed sometime after midnight and to rest on Sunday. Nobody in Paris thinks of either proposition. The only difference between Paris at midnight and Paris at midday is that it is livelier at midnight. The performance is continuous and it is worth the price of admission.

Coming into a country where your language is not generally spoken is always a little trying on the nerves. The French people have made it as easy as possible, but the ways are strange and the helpless tourist can only do as others do and trust to Providence and the power of a little money distributed as well as possible. I do not know how much Providence has had to do with it, but I do believe there are mighty few doors in France which a piece of money will not unlock. When I came into France I knew only two French expressions, one meaning "How much?" and the other, "Thank you." With that vocabulary we went through the custom-house examination, a five-hour railroad journey, landed in a big city station, got a carriage, reached the hotel and an interpreter without any more trouble than we would have in Sterling. Of course everybody from conductor to porter knew we were Americans and could not speak French, knew what we ought to do next and showed the way, and all we had to do was to look pleasant and hand out small change. And it doesn't cost much to be liberal in France. I gave the conductor an equivalent to our 10 cents, and I know he thought I was rich. The porter who took my baggage through the custom-house and brought me a carriage was deeply impressed with my financial standing when I gave him 6 cents worth of French coppers. The coachman who brought Mrs. Morgan and myself with four big grips from the station to the hotel, two miles, charged me the full price, 30 cents for everything, and when I tossed him another dime like a millionaire he took his hat off three times. The French people I have met have been very polite. They always tip their hats and go out of their way to show me, and they are never so discourteous as to refuse 2 cents. Imagine giving a Santa Fe conductor 10 cents for showing you where to sit in the car!

As a lesson in political economy I will put in my observation so far as I have gone: Everything in Europe that is made or done by labor is cheap. I was offered a tailor-made suit of clothes in London for $18 that would cost $30 in Hutchinson. A farm laborer in England gets about 50 cents a day and boards himself. The barber shaves you for 2 or 3 cents. Bread and meat are higher than in the United States. You can see how the wage-earner gets it going and coming. I am learning a few things from experience that I had been told before, but I want to visit a few more places before I try to form my conclusions and put them into print.

Paris is a beautiful city. In spite of the great business houses, the manufactories and the banks which I have seen, it strikes me as a kind of play town. Every day in the week in Paris looks like an American town on the Fourth of July, and on Sunday it is Fourth of July and Christmas together and then some. The men who are working at wages that would make Americans vicious, are as light-hearted and pleasant appearing as a Sunday school picnic. The women are as vivacious as a lot of school ma'ams at institute. As soon as work is completed it seems as if every Parisian only goes home to put on his good clothes and then comes down town accompanied by his wife, or somebody's wife. Half the places of business along the principal streets are restaurants and a good many of the others are also restaurants. The Frenchman sits at a little table on the sidewalk in front of the café and puts in the evening drinking one glass of wine or absinthe, chatting with his neighbor and watching the women go by with their good clothes and bright faces. Every French woman is an artist when it comes to clothes. The goods may not cost much, but the gown is tastefully made, and if the lady wants to she sticks on a bow or jabs a flower in her hat, regardless of every rule except that it looks pretty there —and it always does. Bright and light gowns, hats that are up-to-date or ahead, hair to match the hat and hose to match the dress— and the artist's work is done. No wonder the men hurry down town and sit on the sidewalk!

In the afternoon and evening the Paris streets look like a spring millinery opening—also like a display of samples of fine hosiery. Perhaps I ought not to go into the subject, but it will not be a fair description of Paris if I leave it out, and I must warn any other Kansan who may venture this way. When a Parisian lady walks along a sidewalk that is perfectly clear and clean she daintily lifts her dress so as to display only the top of the shoe, maybe an inch or two more. Sometimes she thoughtlessly raises the gown a little higher. When she reaches the street-crossing—but I had better stop, for she doesn't. I have always been of the opinion that under such circumstances a plain, respectful man should look the other way and I have a crick in my neck from looking—the other way— since I came to Paris. Remember this is in fine weather when the walks and crossings are clean. "They say" that when the walks are muddy the result is even more startling to a staid observer from Kansas. If the weather gets bad I don't know what I will do.

IN PARIS: LOOKING THE OTHER WAY.

The philosophy in the above is that it gives you an idea of Paris with its brilliantly lighted streets, the men eating and drinking, sitting at the little tables along the walks, the well-dressed people, the brilliant colors, the laughter, the bright and polite conduct of men and women, the holiday appearance, the pleasure that everyone is having, and the general gait at which Parisians travel. As another example let me add, fully one-third of that part of Paris which in any other city would be devoted to business, is given up to public gardens, playgrounds for children, parks and drives,—not out in the country or to one side, but right through the center of Paris. The houses, business and residence, are none of them more than six stories high, and I am told the law does not permit higher structures. It is a good idea, for you get air and sunlight, which you often do not in New York and Chicago, and you can occasionally see out over the city. About every so often is a circle or square from which radiate from six to a dozen avenues and boulevards. These streets divide into others which reach forward to other squares, and are intersected at every conceivable angle by cross-streets. The object of this plan was to place artillery in the square and thus command the streets and boulevards against the revolutionists, who have always been doing or about to do something in Paris. The houses, five or six stories high, are built right up from the sidewalk, and have inner courts. Usually there are stores or shops in the downstairs rooms facing the street and living-rooms back and above. And speaking of stores, most of them are about ten by twelve feet, one-half display window. The interior is lined with mirrors which make the room look large and two or three customers like a crowd. The French use mirrors every chance—there are three beautiful mirrors in our small bedroom. The shops are generally decorated with flowers, pictures and statuary and a sign "English spoken," the latter being usually a delusion and a snare. Instead of naming a street or avenue and then sticking to it, the names of the streets frequently change. The boulevard our hotel is on begins as the Madeleine, runs two blocks and then becomes the Capoucins, two blocks more and it is the Italiens. We are on the Capoucins part, and besides the Boulevard des Capoucins, there is street "Rue des Capoucins," and a square "Place des Capoucins," each in a different section. The necessity of a stranger in Paris keeping sober is very apparent. The streets, squares and public buildings are adorned with frequent statues—good ones. Almost any way you turn there is something beautiful to look at. The French are artists and lovers of art. If there were such a thing as a Kansas joint in Paris it would be decorated like an art gallery. But the joints in Paris are open and run twenty-four hours a day, seven days in the week, and the police never interfere with anything that goes on except in case of a disturbance of the peace or abuse of the government.

The French like Americans and don't like the English or the Germans. But that does not mean they refuse anybody's money. In our country when a man gets a comfortable income he grows gray-haired and wrinkled trying to make more. A Frenchman spoke to me of this trait, and said that when one of his countrymen reached the point where he could live nicely on what he had accumulated or the salary he was receiving, he quit worrying and took to the cafés and boulevards to enjoy life. Perhaps the French way is the best, at least the French look happier over mighty little than we do over much more. They go in for "pleasure" and they enjoy it as do no other people I have seen.

PARIS AND PARISIANS.

PARIS, June 20, 1905.

Almost the first thing we did after we reached Paris was to go to the Place de la Concorde, where the guillotine did its bloody work during the French Revolution. It is now a beautiful square adorned with statues, and is the center of the pleasure-ground of Paris. After tightly shutting our eyes so as to avoid seeing the gay Parisians passing by, we recalled the terrible scenes which took place a little more than a hundred years ago. Here Louis XVI., the unfortunate king, paid the penalty for the crimes of his family and class. Here Marie Antoinette was executed, and scores and hundreds of the French nobility. Poor Marie Antoinette, who always did and said the wrong thing, has been the recipient of the sympathy of the world. But in addition to the sorrow for her I have never been able to get over my sympathy for the thousands of women who marched to Versailles and when the king and queen appeared to quiet them, cried, "Give us bread for our children!" For France at that time was suffering as no other nation has suffered from physical oppression and poverty resulting from misgovernment and utter disregard of the lives and property of the people. In order to carry on wars and build monuments and palaces and indulge in personal dissipation and pleasure, the rulers of France had sucked the life of the nation like the juice from an orange. The French still make a great fuss over Louis XIV., "The grand monarch," who made France the leading nation of Europe. But it was the logical outcome of his methods and grinding government that resulted in the degradation of the people, their poverty and distress, and the revolution which sent his great grandson to the block.

After the French Jacobins executed their king and queen they began to fall out and "revolute" against each other, and so nearly all the leaders of the revolution went to the guillotine and got it where Louis and Antoinette did—in the neck. In a little more than two years over 2,800 persons perished here by the guillotine, and the place is very appropriately called "de la Concorde." Around the square are statues representing eight of the cities of France, the one for Strassburg still there, but draped in black and with emblems of mourning for the city and province taken from France by Germany at the end of the last war. Every Frenchman has in his heart the intent to lick the Germans and recover Alsace.

I will not attempt to describe in detail the great palaces of the Tuileries and the magnificent gardens, the Louvre with its acres of paintings and statuary, most of which I did not see because it was like eating pie—there is a limit. These are historic grounds, for back and forth among statues of peace and beautiful works of art the French people have fought each other time and again, sometimes destroying but always rebuilding. From Place de la Concorde extends the Champs-Elysées (pronounced Shame-on-Lizzy, as near as I can get it). This is a great avenue 400 yards wide and over a mile long, consisting of parallel boulevards running through trees and flowers, playgrounds and palaces here and there, and at all times of the day and night filled with people and carriages.

The Champs-Elysées and the Bois de Boulogne, a park of over 2,000 acres in which it terminates, are the fashionable drives of Paris. It cost only 40 cents an hour for Mrs. Morgan and I to drive with the Parisian élite, and we took advantage of the opportunity to see Paris society. The carriages in the early evening extend in procession over miles of boulevard, and are often six or eight abreast. The drives wind around through woods, by good-sized lakes, along sides of cascades, and the carriages are filled with the swellest lot of gowns and cutest little dogs I have ever seen. Nearly every woman has a dog on her string as well as a man. In all of this style there is a general lack of formality which is appropriate to the scenery. It is not an uncommon sight to see the ladies and gentlemen with their arms around each other. It isn't so bad when you get used to it, and the fashion is considered strictly proper in France. I am no longer shocked when I see a young man just ahead of me in the street put his arm around his girl, and in the street cars and automobiles the sight is a frequent one and never attracts comment or disapproval. At first Mrs. Morgan and I nudged each other at such things, but in less than a week's time the novelty has disappeared.

I like the Champs-Elysées, for it looks a good deal as First avenue in Hutchinson would if it were about ten times as wide and the city kept up the parking.

And that leads me to repeat an observation which I have made before. It takes a strong government to do big things. You couldn't get the people in America to put up money to construct palaces, widen boulevards, set up statues in all directions and devote the main part of the city to trees, flowers, walks and drives, playgrounds and art galleries. But whether the government of France has been a monarchy or a republic has made no difference in the fact that it exercised nearly absolute power over such things. The government appoints the officials in all cities and provinces and the government has the army. We talk about "government ownership" as if it were something new. The government of France has been in business more than a century. For example, the government has the monopoly of the tobacco business— manufactures and sells all the tobacco used in France, charges what it pleases and puts out mighty poor stuff. The government has owned the Sèvres china decorating factory for over a century, and the Gobelin tapestry, and I don't know how many more such things. Lack of knowledge of the language has kept me from finding out all on these subjects I am going to before I get home, but it seems to me that whenever the French government sees some exceptionally profitable business, it just takes hold of the proposition and passes a law forbidding anyone else competing. The French are used to this sort of thing and accept it as the inevitable. I wonder if Americans would stand for it and for all the petty regulations that go with it. An army of workingmen is required to maintain all these parks, palaces, art galleries, opera-houses and government institutions, and I suspect the number is never reduced. A friend was telling how in a short ride on a government railroad his ticket was examined by five conductors. We reached the conclusion that this work, which in America would have been done by one man, was strung out for the good political reason—more jobs. Of course nothing like that would happen in America.

The workingmen still wear the long blouse outside the trousers, which looks like a heavy night-shirt and reaches below the knees. At the time of the great revolution the workingmen were so poor that they could not afford to wear trousers and the long blouses were all that covered them. Hence came the nickname "sanscullottes," meaning "without breeches," and as all who have read the story of the revolution or Victor Hugo's books will remember, the Sansculottes, the men without breeches, made up the mob which upset the throne and established the republic.

The French still worship Napoleon. They have forgiven the sacrifice of blood and treasure which he forced from them, and remember the glory and the greatness of the empire. And in spite of the fact that Napoleon III. quit the emperor business under a cloud, having been removed from office after his surrender to the Germans in 1870, he is well thought of, for during his reign France and Paris prospered and times were good. There is a large party in France that favors the return of the present representative of the Napoleon family, Prince Victor, to the throne. We went to the Church of Madeleine, the most beautiful and fashionable church in Paris, and over the altar is a beautiful painting of Napoleon receiving the crown from the pope, with Christ in the background of the picture. That is just like the French.

I made an effort to get into the meeting of the Chamber of Deputies, the French congress, but failed. You have to have a ticket of admission, and it must be applied for several days in advance. They tell me the session is a good deal like an old-time Kansas Populist convention, where everybody said what he wanted to and then everybody was of the same opinion still. The meeting often gets so tumultuous that the president of the body adjourns it. Such an assembly must be guarded by careful and tactful leadership or it will end in a row. I can't understand French politics. There are really no parties such as we have. A large majority favor the republic. The minority is composed of Clericals, Bonapartists, Radicals, and Socialists. The government party is divided into factions, and the issues are personal rather than on economic questions. The minority is of course divided, and the result is that the government wins somehow or other nearly every time. If it should lose, a new cabinet would be formed; but that would be taken from the same party as the old, and would be merely a different lot of statesmen. The French republic is all right so long as there is no serious trouble, but a Dreyfus incident, or a war, or hard times might overturn the government, and nobody knows whether the monarchists might not get on top again. The church is opposed to the policy of the republic, which has been to decrease the power of the church, cut off the parochial schools, and take education out of the hands of the religious bodies. The men in France are not very religious, leaving that part of life to the women and children. But a large and respectable party is in opposition to the government on account of the way it has confiscated church property and driven out the religious orders.

There are only a few electric lines in Paris, and they are not in the main part of the city. The people use carriages a great deal, for they are so cheap; and also omnibuses. The usual means of traveling in the city, aside from the cab, is the omnibus, which is double-decked, carrying as many people on top as inside. This seems a trifle slow to Americans, but it works all right in Paris. The 'buses make regular processions up and down the principal streets, and as they are nearly always filled inside and outside, they add immensely to the Parisian picture. There is an underground railroad and there are dummy lines in the suburbs, but I think the people of Paris like to travel where they can see and be seen. The cabs are victorias. Automobiles are everywhere, and if you go to Paris to live and want to cut any ice you must get one.

I saw a little scene which seemed to show up Parisian character. A cab collided slightly with another. Immediately both drivers were off their vehicles, gesticulating and talking about 300 words a minute. As they shook their fists and grew red in the face with the words that came so fast they interfered with each other, I thought somebody would surely be killed. Nobody noticed them. No one paid any attention. And finally the two exhausted men climbed back to their places and drove on. I know they used French words to each other that in America would have ensured a police court trial for disturbance of the peace. A French friend to whom I mentioned the matter said it was the invariable way, and he thought the French method of taking out their wrath in words was better than the American way of fighting it out. Perhaps he was right, but as I afterward saw the scene repeated in different forms it always occurred to me that it was childish. And that reminds me to say that the Frenchman is in the habit of playing with his children, taking part in their games as excitedly as they do.

The French people are industrious and they save their money. France is really a rich nation. Most of the money is made in what seem small ways to Americans. The French are what we call "thrifty." No matter how little they earn they save something, and the whole family works,—men, women and children. When their day's labor is ended the whole family goes out for a good time—cheap, or within their means. Their natural temperaments and the beautiful surroundings make it easy for them to do this, and it is very seldom a Frenchman leaves his native land. He doesn't travel much, but he believes in other people traveling and coming to France to spend their money. He is willing to help in the good work of separating foreigners from their cash, but he is gentlemanly about it. I like the French people even though I can't understand some of the ways their minds work.

RURAL FRANCE.

MARSEILLES, FRANCE, June 23, 1905.

Rural France is a picture. Seen from a car-window it is a succession of fields and villages, at this time of year a continuous combination of greens and white. French farms are small. I suppose twenty or thirty acres is a big place, and many are much less than that. But the land is fertilized, drained, irrigated and worked to the limit. The people live in villages and not much on their own farms. Each village has a common pasture. During the day the farmers go out onto their little places and in the evening they return to town to spend the hours with their neighbors and friends. The houses are all white stone with red tiled roofs and the villages are numerous, one every two or three miles in every direction. A farm of twenty acres is divided into strips for various crops, so that the landscape is striped with the fields of wheat, alfalfa, potatoes and grass, which seem to be the popular products. Cattle are not so numerous, but sheep are plentiful, goats abound and hogs (always white that I have seen) are on every place. A strip of land a hundred yards wide in wheat will run across the twenty acres, and the next strip will be some other crop, making the hues of green vary. The most extensive crop besides grass is grapes, and hillsides which in our country would be considered too steep and too stony for cultivation are covered with vines. Nature is like the French, artistic when she has a chance, and the combination produces a beautiful effect. Coming from Paris to Marseilles through the valleys of the Seine and the Rhone, it was 500 miles of continuous agriculture and pretty towns. Do you wonder it looks like a picture, with the villages of white houses and red tops, the fields and hills of green, and the rivers like ribbons running here and there?

France is ahead of England and Ireland in this point: Nearly every French farmer owns his own place, even if it is small. In Great Britain the big landlords own the land and rent it to tenants. In France the farmers, or peasants, as they are called, are landlords of their own if it is small. The French nobility lost their possessions and they were bought up by the people. A French farmer does not have the opportunity to make himself a large land proprietor. He can work all his days and only hope to accumulate a little place and enough to take care of him in his last days. But he is able to do that, and it has been almost impossible to do so in Great Britain.

The farms are separated from one another by high stone walls. In driving along the highway these walls shut off the view of the fields and you have to get up above the walls to see the picture. The stone walls are the evidence that the place is the exclusive property of the owner. The grass field is inclosed by these high fences, and the gates are locked at night as if they were afraid somebody would steal the land. It looks strange indeed to a tourist from the land of quarter-sections and barb wires.

Every Frenchman has to serve in the army three years. This is not militia service, but regular soldiery. It takes three of the best years out of a young man's life. Of course it gives some compensation in the way of discipline, and in continental Europe every nation has to keep its pockets full of rocks and its people ready for war with the neighbors. A republic cannot neglect this matter any more than a monarchy, and France loses a great deal by the withdrawal of its young men from the producing class during a time when they could be very useful.

In the fields men and women work side by side. The women of France have plenty of rights. They can plow or rake hay all day long, and then they can indulge in the recreation of housework in the evening. This is harvest-time, and on nearly every farm I saw the whole family at work, not with reapers and mowers, but with good sickles and hand-rakes. The women seem to age earlier than in America, but this fact is true wherever I have been outside of the United States.

That reminds me of a mistaken notion I had before coming here. I thought the women of the United States were more active in a business way than the women of other countries, and had progressed in taking hold of what is generally called "men's work" more than the women of Europe. That is a mistake. Proportionately women have more to do with business in England and France than they do in America. Nearly all the hotels in Great Britain are managed by women. Shops, stores and offices are filled with women. The fact is, the combined labor of husband and wife is necessary among "the great plain people," to get enough to support the family, and in Ireland, England and France this is taken as a matter of course. Especially in France do I find women managing business, and doing so with the skill and success which shows that it is neither a new thing nor a side occupation. In America it is generally accepted that a man who can do so will take the brunt of the work and a woman will find her time fully occupied with housekeeping. And there is also a widespread practice of raising the girls to sit in the parlor while their mother washes the dishes. That is not the way they do in France. A young woman is brought up to expect what she will get—a young man whom she will have to help, or they will go hungry. There are not many chances for a young man to get ahead fast. He has no reason to believe that he will be better fixed than his father or than his grandfather. In fact, in France a boy usually follows the occupation of his father, so that a family for generations will be farmers, shoemakers, shopkeepers, etc. In America a farmer usually wants his son to study law, while a lawyer hopes his son will be a business man, and a merchant sees the advantage of rural life. Our people change around from generation to generation, and I doubt on that account if we make as good workmen as the French do, who are brought up in their occupation. Of course our people would be discontented with the French way, but the Frenchmen seem to be satisfied and they get a good many compensating advantages to offset the opportunities which young Americans have, but of which young Frenchmen never dream.

There are some disadvantages under which these Europeans labor which they should remove. They never get any pie. Here in a land where the cherries grow big and red and juicy, a Frenchman will grow to manhood and old age without knowing the taste of cherry pie. It is a great misfortune. Since landing in Europe I have never seen a piece of pie of any description, from Queenstown to Marseilles. They have "tarts" and "sweetmeats," but these can't approach pie any more than Cow creek can be compared to the Mississippi river. Even in the best hotels and restaurants of London there is no sign of pie on the bill of fare, and the French cooks, who can make old hash taste like choice bits of fresh meat or better, have not learned the science of constructing pie, mince, apple, pumpkin, cherry or any kind of pie. I do not know how they do it, but the railroad restaurants are run without pie. Even the crowned heads go through life without knowing the taste of pumpkin pie, and one of my ideas of royalty in my early days was that a king or prince could have custard pie with flaky brown crust three times a day. No wonder the rulers of Europe are afraid of revolution. If they would see that their subjects had square meals and pie at least for dinner, the heads that wear the crowns need not be so uneasy.

And the Europeans are trying to live without hot cakes for breakfast. I suppose there is not a man or woman in Europe who would recognize by experience the rich and regal buckwheat cake, or the corn cake, or the pancake. I can't understand why the reformers in this country do not get to the point, and see that the people have flapjacks for breakfast as well as pie for dinner, and then let the disbanding of the armies proceed.

Every American citizen who is sane and patriotic believes that he is a fisherman, and tries to prove it whenever he gets near a creek or river. Whether he actually catches any fish or not, he "goes fishing." I was somewhat worked up in Ireland and England because the streams were nearly all private property and the ordinary citizen had no chance to fish any more than he did to attend the wedding of the prince. I was glad to know that it is different in France. Last Sunday in Paris we walked along the banks of the Seine as it runs through the city between the stone walls and under the stone bridges. The stream was lined with fishermen. One of the privileges the citizens of Paris enjoy is to fish in the Seine, and I was told that there were at least 10,000 Frenchmen watching the corks on the river that afternoon. I waited for a long time to see them catch a French fish. Occasionally one of the men or women would pull up a line, but the bait was never missing. Finally I asked a friend who has been in Paris some time if anybody ever caught a fish. He said he had never really heard of anyone but there was a tradition that along about the time of Napoleon III. somebody did catch a fish in the Seine. He doubted the story, but said I could believe it if I wanted to. And yet there are theologians and doctors of divinity who say the French people are losing in faith, when these thousands were demonstrating to the contrary and were heartily enjoying the privilege the government gives and for which the Parisians would doubtless fight, the right to fish in the river.

This city of Marseilles, in which we are spending a couple of days, is the principal seaport of France. It was established by the Phœnicians, and was an important town when Julius Cæsar was setting up the primaries in Rome. It is the port from which France does business with southern Europe, Africa, Asia, and even America. Consequently the harbor is full of all kinds of shipping, the streets are crowded with Arabs, Greeks, Spaniards, Turks, Italians, and representatives of all nations which use the sea, and the town has the largest collection of odors and smells that I have met. As a strange fact I will add that Marseilles is the first large city I have visited in Europe with a good up-to-date electric railway system. Americans do not come here very much. So far as I know, Mrs. Morgan and I are the only Americans in the city, and there is not a soul at our hotel who can speak English. So you see we are running up against a little real foreign experience.

ITALY.

GETTING INTO ITALY.

ROME, June 27, 1905.

One can hardly realize until he has had some experience how quick and how decided is the transition from one country to another, and especially the change in language. At 5 o'clock yesterday afternoon we were in France, everybody around us and on the train talking French. At 6 o'clock we were in Italy: everybody was talking Italian, and the French language had disappeared as quickly as did the English when we landed at Calais. You know when you are going from one country to the next, also, because the custom-house is on the line and you have to haul out all your dirty clothes and souvenirs for the officials to examine to see if you are a smuggler. Let me tell how we came into Italy.

We boarded the train on the French railroad at Monte Carlo and had an hour's ride to the frontier. By this time I had picked up enough French so I could get along reasonably well with the help of the sign language and a little money. But neither of us knew a word of Italian, and there was no one with us that day who could talk English. At Vintimille, where we crossed the line, we had to change trains, have our tickets signed and our baggage examined in forty minutes. With a full realization that nobody could understand me and I could understand no one, I tackled the job, putting my trust in Providence and a pocketful of small Italian coins which I had secured at Monte Carlo. When the train stopped in the Vintimille station a porter came alongside and according to the custom of the country I handed the four "bags" which constitute our baggage to him through the car-window. Then we got out and I told him in English what I wanted. He reeled off a lot of Italian and two or three bystanders chipped in, and a hotel runner attempted to capture us. But I took out my through ticket, pointed to it, jingled the coins in my pocket, and the porter understood. Of course I did not know at first whether he did or not, but we followed him and he led us into the custom-house and put our grips on a big table. Up came an inspector and jabbered Italian and I jabbered back in English. We both laughed, and of course neither understood what the other wanted. He asked me several questions, to all of which I said, "Can't understand," and then he gave me a final grin and said, "Tobac?" To that I said "No," and shook my head. Without looking into the grips at all he chalked something on them which I suppose corresponds to our "O. K.," threw up his hands and said something to the porter which made him and the surrounding onlookers burst forth in a loud guffaw. I felt as I suppose a poor Dago does when he strikes America. I again showed my ticket to the porter and pointed to the place where it must be signed. He puzzled over that a while and then took it and went away for a few minutes and came back with the work properly done. Then he took us to the Italian train the other side of the station, put our bags in the racks and we hoped we were on the right train—we were. I gave that porter a lot of Italian money, aggregating about 20 cents American, and he saluted me as if I were a duke or a saint. Mrs. Morgan says I spoiled him with my extravagant tip. But I felt so grateful to him that I didn't care if I did make him proud with all that money at once. Let him swell up inside and parade the avenue all the evening and take his family out to dinner if he wants to. Let him take that 20 cents and pose as an Italian Rockefeller.

Then we were in Italy and couldn't even read the signs. It makes you foolish to look over the door of your car and see the words which mean "Smoking permitted," or "Smoking forbidden" and not know which. We were the only people in the compartment, and the conductor took a great deal of interest in us. He tried to tell us something and I tried to tell him something, but when we got through neither of us had added to our stock of knowledge. After the train had been going for a while he came to us and began to make signs and chatter. He held up both hands with the fingers extended. Mrs. Morgan was quite sure he meant $10 fine for smoking in that compartment, so I threw away my cigar, but he didn't stop. At last I realized that he was making the signs of a man eating and drinking. I guessed he meant by both hands that the train would stop ten minutes for lunch, or that we wouldn't get anything to eat until 10 o'clock. When the train stopped at the next station it turned out that the first of these two was right.

The road from Vintimille to Genoa is a branch, and the ticket had to be signed and trains changed again at Genoa, and we also wanted to get a sleeping-car on to Rome. We had twenty-seven minutes at the station in Genoa, which is bigger than the Union Depot at Kansas City. Again I threw the grips out of the window and followed the porter. Then I left Mrs. Morgan with the baggage while the porter led me a merry chase around the block to the office where the ticket was to be signed or "viséd." It was 11 o'clock at night, and you can imagine how it felt to be guided around among those Italians wondering all the while if the porter knew what I wanted. But he did and I returned in safety, and then I tried to find out about the sleeping-car. In French this is called a "Litts-salon," and in German a "Schlaf-wagen," literally a sleep-wagon. I tried English, French and German, but finally found the sleeper by examining the train,—next to the engine, of course, just where I wasn't expecting it. We got on board safely, and after distributing a lot more Italian coppers I found we had transacted the business and had five minutes to spare,—as good time as I could have made in America to do all those things. All I then had to do was to hand out the required sleeper fare, $7.50 to Rome, 300 miles, three times what Mr. Pullman would have charged. But I reserve my comments on European sleeping-cars until I get a little more experience for a letter on railroads in the Old World.

And this is an old world. When I was in Boston I looked with awe upon the churches and monuments of 1776. In England these years seemed recent, and it took a cathedral or a castle of Elizabeth's time or back to William the Conqueror. But here in Rome the very latest and newest buildings that we look at are those of the early Christians, and to get a real thrill they have to show me something B. C. It is really a good deal like living back in those times. I can't read the newspapers and don't know what has happened since I left Paris nearly a week ago. At that time the Russians and Japs were either going to have a conference or a fight, or both. Sometimes I wonder what has occurred, but generally I am concerning myself with what Julius Cæsar did, standing by the old forum and imagining Mark Antony denouncing the boss-busters, or wondering if Cicero's speech against Catiline was not a political blunder which would make the old man trouble at the next city election. The only difficulty is to make the modern Italians fit in with the old Romans. Somehow or other it is hard to imagine the lazy gents who hold out their hands for coppers as real Romans who ruled the world.

The first real striking feature of Italy we noticed at Vintimille was the policemen. They wear handsome full-dress uniforms with red braid down the trousers, gilt lace and epaulets on the coats, tri-cornered hat with an immense plume, and carry in sight a sword and revolver. An Italian policeman walking his beat makes a gorgeous Knight Templar uniform look cheap. You never see one policeman—there are always two together. The police of the whole country are appointed by the royal government, not by local officials, and are selected from the army. They are good-looking fellows, and wear their tight, heavy coats buttoned up in front regardless of the fact that it is Italy and the climate is not better than Kansas the last of June. One of the troubles with Italy is that it is really a second-class power, but it tries to keep up an army and navy in rivalry with Germany, Russia, and France. Every Italian must put in three years in active service. Take a country about the size of Kansas, fill it up with an army of 300,000 men and you see soldiers in every direction. Immense cathedrals and palaces filled with valuable gems and works of art, an army of expensive uniforms, and a poverty-stricken people,—that is Italy. The tourist hurries along and shuts his eyes to the distress as much as he can, visits the galleries and the churches, the ruins and the historic spots. He tries to see only the Italy of 2,000 years ago. He is fortunate if he can keep himself worked up in an ecstasy over the Cæsars and the old masters, so that the half-clothed children, the broken-down women and the men working without hope, do not leave an impression on his heart. I can't shut my eyes tight enough to avoid seeing those things and sympathizing with the poor Italian people who have no show.

But here we are in Italy, not the Italy of to-day, but the Italy of Cæsar and Cicero, Nero and Constantine, the Italy where Paul and Peter planted the Christian religion and where they died the death of martyrs; the Italy of temples and colosseums, cathedrals and catacombs,—the Italy we read about, if you please, and not the Italy now on the map.

ROME AND ROMANS.

Rome, June 29, 1905.

There is so much in the point of view. Here are things which I have studied about, read about, wondered about. Some of them on close inspection are impressive yet. Others are commonplace. And there are even some which are ridiculous. On approaching Rome I had tried to take an inventory of the things I most wanted to see first: The Forum, St. Peter's, the Appian Way, the Coliseum, the Sistine Chapel, the Tarpeian Rock, the Vatican, and the list was as long as I could set down. But really the words that kept haunting me and which were always in my mind were "the yellow Tiber." Like every other school-boy of my time, I had learned and recited "Horatius at the Bridge," and I wanted to see the raging torrent which saved Rome when Horatius held back the foe until the Romans had cut down the only bridge. I kept saying to myself:

"Then up spake brave Horatius,

The captain of the gate:

'To every man upon this earth

Death cometh soon or late;

And how can man die better

Than when facing fearful odds,

For the ashes of his fathers

And the temples of his gods?'"

THE ITALIAN NOBLEMAN OF THE STAGE, AND THE REAL THING

Accordingly the first observation I made in Rome was of the Tiber. It is yellow, all right, and about as wide as the Cottonwood river. It seemed impossible to associate that stream with the Tiber of which historians had told and poets sung. But it was the Tiber, all right—from another view-point.

Now with St. Peter's it was different. I have seen some right nice churches in America, but of course they do not come up to European cathedrals. St. Paul's in London was disappointing, and Notre Dame in Paris was not up to the advance advertising. But when it comes to impressiveness St. Peter's at Rome is to my mind the greatest imaginable. It is so big and yet so proportioned, so grand and yet so substantial, so full of precious memories of martyrs and divines and so tastefully and magnificently decorated with pictures that tell the story of the faith it stands for. All the people in Hutchinson could worship in one side of St. Peter's, and yet there is none of that barny, barracksy look which usually goes with great size and capacity. The length is 232 yards, the transept is 150 yards and the height of the nave 151 feet, the dome is 435 feet to the cross. But figures don't tell anything about St. Peter's. The interior is tapestry and painting, gold without tinsel, pictures without tawdry effect, and columns that add and do not detract from the dignity of the structure. Under the great dome is the tomb of Peter, the disciple who made so much trouble, but knowing his energy and power, whom Christ made the rock upon which the church was to be built.

Next door to St. Peter's is the Vatican, where the pope resides, and the first thing we saw there was the Sistine Chapel. Here is where my view-point differs from most people. I concede that the paintings in the Sistine Chapel are beautiful, especially in their design and their color. The old masters who did the work under the direction of Michael Angelo have never been equaled in their ability to make rich color. But I contend that the subject of a picture should count as well as the drawing and the color. When Michael Angelo attempted to paint God Almighty he couldn't do it. The color is all right and the proportions are perfect, but all that Michael Angelo did was to paint a man a little larger than Adam, and that does not come up to my ideal of the Divine. The fact is that neither Michael Angelo nor anyone else can put onto canvas such a subject, and therefore Michael should not have tried it. His fault was in his judgment of what can be painted. The entire effect of the remainder of the beautiful ceilings and walls with their paintings of scenes from Old and New Testament, was spoiled for me when I couldn't get away from that central figure, that failure of ability to do the impossible.

I would like to have the support of the women-folks in my theory in regard to the failure of the Sistine Chapel, so I will add that in the picture where Michael paints the devil, he makes the devil half snake and the upper half a woman. If I remember correctly, the great painter was an old bachelor,—probably not one of his own motion.

The paintings mix up the pagan with the Christian. "The Last Judgment" has Christ the central figure as judge, surrounded by apostles and saints, and the hell part of the painting is according to Dante, with the old Roman idea of the boatman Charon ferrying the lost across the river. In this picture Michael Angelo made a hit. He put the face of an enemy of his, an officer of the pope, on the painting of Minos, one of the leading devils of hell. The offending official had objected to some of the artist's work on account of the nudity of the figures, and Michael has sent him down the ages as the face of a devil.

But there is no call for me to describe paintings and statuary and cathedrals. A hasty sketch like this is not giving them fair treatment. You can't go anywhere in Rome without running into something beautiful or something historic. Go down a street and there will be the baths of Diocletian, turn around and there will be the Forum, and next is the Coliseum, the Arch of Constantine, Trajan's forum and column, the Palace of Tiberius, the Stadium, and so on until you can't rest with the long list of things you saw and ought to remember, and some that you ought to have seen but didn't because you were just too tired to look around. The Forum, the Coliseum and all this kind of things look just like the pictures, and they are there,—that's all I can say about them, although the feeling of actually having seen and touched is one of a great deal of satisfaction and worth going to Rome to have.

I don't know how many churches there are in Rome. There are eighty dedicated to the Virgin and fully as many to St. Peter. They are filled with great paintings and statuary. Rome is the center of the greatest Christian church, and for centuries the civilized world, or a large part of it, has sent its gifts to the temples and shrines. Thousands and tens of thousands of young men are studying here for the priesthood. The streets are filled with their black gowns and hats. Here and there along the streets and roads are shrines erected to patron saints. All the churches are open seven days in the week, and there are always people in them at their devotions.

As a contrast to the power and greatness of the present church we went to see the catacombs, the burrows in the earth to which the Christians of the early centuries fled for safety, and in which they buried their dead. The catacombs of St. Calixtus, which we visited are said to contain twelve miles of underground passages. Along the sides and in the occasional niches and chapels are the places where the bodies were put. The passages go down thirty to forty feet and the catacombs are from four to six stories downward, just as a building is that much above ground. In these places the early Christians kept alive their faith under the terrible persecution of the emperors. Amid the tombs they met and worshipped in spite of imperial decree and certain death if captured. Rude pictures and inscriptions on the walls tell part of the story which has made the world wonder ever since as the Roman government did then, at the power of the faith for which men and women would so live and so die.

Coming out of the catacombs we drove along the Appian Way, the great military road constructed over 300 years B. C. I had expected to have a good thrill of enthusiasm over the Appian Way, but somehow it did not come. The Appian Way is an ordinary good country road lined with old houses, wine gardens, ruins and high fences. There are still a number of villas and palaces, but the owners are poor and the basements are usually rented out for stables and the upper apartments for tenements. Italian noblemen are generally poor, and if they have palaces are obliged to rent rooms and keep boarders.

Another cherished hope of mine is gone. I had read about the beautiful Italian peasant girls and have seen them on the stage singing in opera and dressed in fetching short skirts and bright-colored bodices. Italian girls work in the fields with the boys and then help their mothers with the children, and most of them look tired and sickly. The fetching skirts hang like loose wall-paper and the "bright bodice" looks as if the girl was wearing her mother's old corset outside her clothes.

The largest and most numerous ruins in Rome are those of the public baths erected by the state and by the emperors. The Romans in those days were sporty, banqueted all night and bathed all next day to get over the effects. But there are no public baths now—at least none of consequence. And judging by the ordinary senses of sight and smell, bathing has become one of the lost arts with a large number of the Romans of to-day.

VENICE, THE BEAUTIFUL.

VENICE, July 3, 1905.

I suppose everybody knows about Venice, the city built in the water. During the sixth century the "barbarians" from the north were overrunning Italy, killing or making slaves of the people and destroying the cities and towns. A number of the inhabitants of northeast Italy fled for safety to a group of small islands in the shallow bay of the Adriatic sea, and there built up little villages which were united in a republic and became the city and suburbs which we call Venice. They naturally were a seafaring and trading people, and Venice was the port of commerce between the Orient and Europe. The Crusades stimulated business, and Venice was the most important trading-point on the Mediterranean. At that time there was no Suez canal and no knowledge of an ocean route to Asia, and all commerce passed through Venice. The little republic grew strong and powerful, captured and retained possessions in Italy and the islands of the Mediterranean. Venice was one of the powers of Europe about the fifteenth century, and thought she had the world by the tail. But the Turks captured Constantinople, other routes to Asia were discovered about the time Columbus reached America, and Venice as a great political power and business center suffered a collapse. In other words, the boom in Venice busted and Venice has never done much on her own account since. The first few hundred years the government was that of a republic, but about the close of the thirteenth century the nobles who had won leadership through trade and war declared their offices hereditary, and thereafter Venice was an aristocracy with a president called "the doge." During the French Revolution the French captured Venice, and then Austria got it, and finally, in 1868, it was united with the kingdom of Italy, where it belongs.

Built on islands, crossed by canals like streets in other cities, without a carriage or a horse, Venice is a strange, and to me, an attractive place. The railroad runs out on a long trestle bridge. It is hardly appropriate to say "landed" in a place like Venice, but we arrived here at ten o'clock at night. The porter for the hotel to which we were going took us through the station and put us into a gondola, and away we went, down back streets and under bridges, with no light except a few corner lamps and the stars. The Venetian gondoliers may be poetical, but their looks do not invite the confidence of the traveler when he intrusts himself to their hands for the first time and late at night. Little chills creep up and down your back as you see the gondola going straight for a corner—sure to hit it, but accidentally doesn't. After you get acquainted with the ways of the city you learn to trust the gondolier, but the first time, late at night, you have your doubts. You may forget just how you arrived in other cities, but not in Venice.

The Grand canal, the main street in Venice, is about seventy-five yards wide and averages sixteen feet deep. The paving question does not bother the city council in Venice. Most of their canal streets are only twelve to thirty feet in width. There are also a few real streets four to ten feet wide, on the inside of the blocks formed by the canals, and the total result is a labyrinth of alleys and canals which are impossible for a stranger to get head or tail of. Along the Grand canal and many others the fine houses of the old prosperous times loom up straight from the water six or seven stories. For example, the front of our hotel, on the Grand canal, has absolutely no sidewalk, only marble steps leading to the water, up which the tide rises about two and a half feet twice a day. The architecture of Venice is Oriental, and is refreshing after the Roman and Greek styles everywhere else in Italy. The churches and public buildings, mostly constructed between the eleventh and fifteenth centuries, have round Moorish towers and are decorated with gold and colors and have very ornate pillars and façades. That makes Venice a beautiful city, and so it is,—if you don't go into the little back alleys where you see the undecorated side. Of the 125,000 people one-fourth have no means of support except charity. In the last few years Venice has revived the glass industry and has developed the lace-making, and times are better than they were. But just think of a people where one-fourth have no chance to earn their living! We visited one of the big lace-making suburbs on the island of Burano. The lace, which Mrs. Morgan says is "b-e-a-u-t-i-f-u-l" and over which all good women rave, is made by girls and women who sit all day on straight-back chairs and labor over the pillow,—and get about twenty-five cents a day wages. We visited the glass-blowers at Murano, the finest in the world, and skilled workmen get up to two dollars a day for a dexterity and ability which would easily command three or four times that amount in America. The people live mostly on fish and vegetables, are very poor and apparently very happy. They are the best-looking folks I have seen in Italy, and evidently enjoy the improvident life which would drive an American to strong drink, or if he were in Italy would drive him to drink the water.

The center of Venice is "the Piazza of St. Mark," a square about two hundred yards long and nearly half as wide, paved with marble and inclosed by fine buildings, including the great Church of St. Mark, the old palace of the doge, the present royal palace, and a glittering array of shops. I should say there were ten thousand beautiful shops in Venice selling lace, glass, art works, beads, curios, pictures, etc. Of course there are not that many, but there seem to be. There is practically nothing else of importance. Venice is a good deal like the world's fair grounds, all glitter and glass, Oriental towers and marble palaces, beautiful bridges and lagoons, and everybody trying to separate the stranger from his money.

Venice is a night town. In the evening the canals are filled with gondolas and everybody is out for a good time. Regular musical clubs drift along with the sweetest Italian opera rendered with real ability, and arias and Italian serenades and love songs until you think the world is nothing but lights glancing on the water, drifting gondolas, song and gladness. Every few minutes one of the singers will pass the hat and you contribute two or three cents and remember you are still on earth. We sit at our hotel and watch the gay crowd in the passing gondolas, or for a few cents get into one, lean back on the easy cushions, smoke a two-cent cigar, and forget all about these poor people with their poverty and their fleas. They have forgotten them themselves.

The patron saint of Venice is St. Mark. In the early days, say a thousand years ago and more, some doge dreamed that Venice would never prosper until the bones of St. Mark were brought here for burial. The bones happened to be in Asia or Africa, and for years the Venetians put in their time fighting the Turks and trying to capture the relics. Finally the bright idea struck them that it would be easier to steal St. Mark's bones than capture them by battle, and an enterprising Venetian merchant did the job. The remains of St. Mark were brought to Venice and a beautiful cathedral with Oriental towers and rich colors built above them. The doge's dream was no fake, for after that Venice prospered greatly. Tradition says that St. Mark used to have a winged lion for a companion, and accordingly the winged lion is the Venetian emblem. The cathedral and the public buildings are full of Oriental works of art captured or stolen from the Turks during the years of the Crusades when Venice was a stronghold of Christendom. Venetian painters have done St. Mark and the lion in every conceivable place, and wherever you go you see his kindly face, the quill pen he used in writing, and the playful winged lion. The only horses in the city are of bronze, and decorate the façade of St. Mark's cathedral. Except for these rather poor imitations I suppose nine-tenths of the people of Venice never saw a horse. Incidentally I will add that it is a great advantage to live in a city where you are not awakened at daylight by the rumble of wagons and carts over stone-paved streets.

The government of Venice during the Middle Ages was something fierce. Nominally a republic, it was controlled by the nobles, who had a general assembly, which selected a senate of seventy-five, of which there was an inner council of ten and a secret tribunal of three, who met masked and did not know each other's identity. If you lived in Venice at that time and had an enemy you wanted to do away with, you would drop a letter accusing him of treason into the letter-box shaped like a lion's head in the counter outside the room of the council of three. It was a pretty sure thing that he would not be heard from again. Of course you would have to do this first, for your enemy might be dropping in a letter while you were thinking about it.

We went through the rooms of the various councils down the secret stairway and over the "Bridge of Sighs," which connected the palace with the prison across the canal street. This was the way the prisoners were brought for trial, and if they went back it was to torture and death. The jails in those times were not built for health or sanitary purposes, and were evidently not examined by the county commissioners. The dungeons are dark and damp, and the guide tells you some awful stories of the rack, the thumbscrew and the block. You can imagine the "good old days" and shudder as you think of the cruelty and the crime. Paraphrasing Byron, who wrote some lines on the subject:

I stood in Venice on the Bridge of Sighs,

Visions of Old from those deep dungeons rise,—

The shrieks of pain, the terrifying cries,

Then I reflect: Perhaps it's mostly lies.

SOME THINGS ON ART.

VENICE, ITALY, July 3, 1905.

Because I have not been writing much to The News on the subject of art, it must not be supposed that I am omitting the regular work of every tourist. Nor do I want it presupposed that I don't know enough about art to tell the difference between a renaissance and a vermicelli. If industry and a desire to thoroughly do the job so it will not have to be done a second time will count for anything, I have been an arduous lover of art in all its forms since I passed the custom-house on the Italian border. Everybody knows that the center of art is Italy and that anything that isn't old and Italian is second-class. When you come to Italy you expect to see the heights of the artistic and you are expected to have fits of ecstasy over the said heights. I have had 'em every time the guidebook told me to. I have endeavored in every way to show that a plain, common citizen of Kansas knew what to do when brought face to face with Raphael, Titian, Michael Angelo and the other gentlemen since whose death the world has never really seen much in art. According to my pedometer I have traveled through 171 miles of cathedrals, 56 miles of public buildings and 85 miles of art galleries —all in ten days. Some people may think my pedometer is too rapid, but I know it is too slow. You know a good bird dog learns never to "set" for anything but a game bird. And it is well established that people with a certain kind of rheumatism can tell the approaching changes in the weather by the twinges in their joints. And it is a fact that even when I do not know there is a cathedral or an art gallery within a hundred miles, let me approach one accidentally and my feet will begin to ache. Then I know what is before me and I try to do my duty. If the work of absorbing Italian art should prove too much for me, the words could be as appropriately put on my tombstone as they were over the early citizen of Dodge who died with a dozen bullets in his body and a half-dozen enemies lying on the floor:

HERE LIES BILL.

HE DONE HIS DAMDEST.

   ANGELS COULD DO

     NO MORE.

There are three places where you always find art in Italy: First and foremost, the churches; second, the public buildings; third, the art galleries and museums. The churches come first, because the Catholic Church has always been the support and promoter of art. For centuries it was the only strong power that encouraged artists. It had the tasteful men of the age and it had the money. The great artists both in painting and sculpture would have had no opportunity and their works would have been destroyed if it had not been for the church. In return, the artists took the subjects of religion and portrayed them most beautifully and effectively. There is hardly a church in Italy which does not have paintings by some of those old painters which would be worth a fortune now if they were for sale. The Catholic faith especially appeals to the artistic sense, and the history of the church furnished a boundless field of subjects. Walls and ceilings of churches are covered with magnificent pictures, the exteriors are decorated with sculpture, and the architecture of the buildings is brilliant and effective. To see paintings, statues or architecture in Italy you first go to the churches, and there you see the greatest and best.

After the churches the art treasures and galleries are found in the public buildings, and there we get what is left of the art of Greece and Rome, together with much of a later time. The old pagan mythology furnished most of the ancient art, together with a few attempts at transferring abstract ideas into concrete form. Of course I don't want to set up as an art critic—I have trouble enough without that. But according to the way I was raised, a large per cent. of ancient sculpture isn't fit to be exhibited to young folks—or to old men. Probably the times were different and fashions in art were acute, but the Grecian and Roman sculptors paid no attention to the rules of common decency as generally understood in this generation. While doing my duty in the art galleries I have actually blushed so much that it grew noticeable to the other art critics, and I fear that I lost standing with them. Of course I am not a regular critic, but I know a few things, and this is one of them.

Another objection I have to the old masters is that they never considered any subject too big for them. I have written something of this when I kicked on Michael Angelo attempting to make a picture of God Almighty. There is too much of that kind of business in Italian art. And another thing is that they couldn't paint good animals. Some of the pictures by the great masters have horses or lions in them, and I believe even the horses would laugh at their own appearance.

Aside from these unimportant objections and a trifling criticism of a great deal of ignorance about drawing and the fitness of things, the "old masters," by which is meant the great painters from about 1400 to 1600, are certainly worthy of their reputation. Everybody I met knew more about art than I did—so they thought—and everyone said: "What wonderful color." The old masters certainly did know how to mix paints so as to make the most beautiful and most lasting colors. I think Titian's red-headed girls are the prettiest reds I have ever seen. Raphael's paintings cannot be criticized by me—their feeling and their execution will make a cynical Kansan stand and admire. Michael Angelo I did not take to so well as I did Titian and Raphael, but he did a lot of work, and he, too, had the ability to make his pictures like life. The other great painters of Italy in these two centuries of the renaissance have not been equaled in any period since, and in spite of the fact that the experience of one generation ought to help the next, I do not believe that the modern Italian painters, or the Englishmen and Americans who go to Italy and copy, can come within several blocks of equaling the work of the "old masters."

There is one more objection I have to the "old masters," and I would like to tell it to their faces. They had the habit of taking a great subject and making it a means of flattery for wealthy patrons. For example, a picture of Christ or the Virgin sitting and talking confidentially with some old scamp of a Medici. Of course I don't blame the old artists. The Medici were a lot of thugs, thieves, highwaymen, murderers, and lovers of art. They put up handsomely for the great masters, and undoubtedly assisted much in promoting art at a time when the princes and nobility of Italy were not respectable according to our standard. This flattery by the old masters may have been necessary to make a living, but I don't think it is Art.

I had one objection which has been overruled on the ground that it was simply because my apprenticeship in art had been too short. Every artist painted a "Madonna." Each had a different ideal or model. Mary was a Jewess. But the Italian artists nearly all ran in pictures of Italians, and each had a different style. It makes a confusing aggregation. I think I have seen a thousand Madonnas, five hundred Magdalens, and from one to three hundred of each of the saints. There is a sameness of subject and a variance in execution which makes me a little nervous. I haven't worked at the art business as long as I should, and therefore I may be too hasty in my judgment, although I am fairly perspiring art at every pore and the climate of Italy in the latter part of June and the first of July has nearly as much cause for perspiration as the climate of Kansas.

AN ITALIAN FOURTH AND SO FORTH.

MENAGIO, ITALY, July 5, 1905.

At an early hour yesterday morning, July 4, we left the hotel in Venice in a gondola, and defiantly waving in the air was an American flag which I carried as proudly and as exuberantly as a ten-year-old boy would at a picnic in Kansas. We met several Americans at the station, and they waved and cheered "Old Glory." We met all kinds of Italians, who looked as amused and curious as a lot of Americans would at an Italian carrying a green, white and red banner down the streets of Hutchinson. I flaunted the stars and stripes in the faces of the Italian policemen, and they seemed to enjoy it. Several people tried to find out from me what it all meant, and in spite of the fact that I told them in good English that this was the Fourth of July, the anniversary of independence, they shook their heads and did not "comprehendo." The weather was very hot and very dry, the train was dusty, and the conditions as near ideal for a successful Fourth of July celebration as could be imagined. The American flag that day floated in the Italian breeze from Venice to Milan and then to Lake Como. The inability to make the Dagoes understand what I meant was embarrassing at times, and I longed vainly for a pack of firecrackers or a few good torpedoes. The conductor on the train was greatly interested. We talked in sign language and all the Italian I knew and all the English he knew, but to no effect. Finally I said the word "liberty," and as the Italian word is about the same, he caught on and I could tell he was approving. "Vive l'America!" I cried, and he took off his hat and said it after me and smiled agreement to the remarks I was making on what the old flag meant. I gave him a big tip, 10 cents,—5 cents for hurrahing for America and 5 cents for listening to my speech.

To-night we are out of the heat of the fertile plains of Lombardy and are in a delightful cool place on the shore of Lake Como, the prettiest and pleasantest place I have seen since we left Killarney. The last part of the day the flag waved over Como, Bellagio, Cernobio, Nesso, Colomo, Bellano, and all the other "o's" that make the list of Italian towns look like the roster of an Irish Fenian society, only the o is at the wrong end of the names.

※ ※ ※

Speaking of "tipping" the conductor reminds me of the tipping system in Italy, which is a subject of the greatest importance to the traveler. I think I have seen only one man in Italy who did not hold out his hand, and that was an armless beggar at the Milan station who had a tin cup in which you were expected to deposit. The tipping custom is general in Europe, but it reaches its greatest development in Italy. Everybody you meet is so courteous and polite, willing to show you or tell you or take you, but always expecting something. You tip the conductor, the porter, the hotel manager, the chambermaid, the "man chambermaid," the elevator boy, the waiter, the head waiter, the clerk, the interpreter, the attendants, the driver, the man who opens the door, the church janitor, the policeman, and everybody you ask a question or who is there to answer if you do ask, and then you tip a few more just because they expect it. This looks like an alarming expenditure of money. But as a matter of fact the total amount of tips is not more than is expected at a big hotel in New York. And when you tip the waiter at the restaurant he does not keep it, but all tips go into a common fund that is divided and is the wages the waiters receive in most cases.

Here is a schedule of "tips," which, after considerable study and comparison with that of others, I have figured as about right:

- Baggageman, 2 cents.
- Elevator boy, 2 cents.
- Chambermaid, 3 cents.
- Man chambermaid, 3 cents.
- Waiter, per day, 5 cents.
- Head waiter, 10 cents.
- Manager of hotel, 20 cents.
- Miscellaneous men and boys, each 1 cent.
- Railroad conductor, 5 cents.
- Policeman, 2 cents.
- Driver, 2 cents.
- Italian nobleman, 3 cents.

- Italian merchant, 2 cents.
- Clerk in store, 1 cent.
- Ordinary civility, 1 cent.

I haven't met the king or queen, but I estimate that if I did and asked a favor they would look like about 30 cents.

The Italian money is like the French money, based on a unit which is equivalent to 20 cents. So when you give a man 10 cents you give him a half-lire or half-franc. The lire is divided into 100 centimes, and when you give a man 2 cents you hand him a great big copper coin with "ten centimes" on it. This small unit of measurement causes an American a peculiar sensation. For example, I had to buy a shirt in Venice and it was marked 5.50. That looked like a big price for a shirt, but reduced to American currency it was only $1.10. I bought some of the long Italian cigars which look like stogies and have straws down the center so they will draw. They were 30 centimes each—only 6 cents American. For a carriage and driver to go anywhere in Rome, carrying Mrs. Morgan and myself and a lot of baggage, it was 1.00, twenty American cents. When two Americans can ride a couple of miles in a comfortable victoria for 20 cents they don't walk much, and they feel as if they were beating somebody and are perfectly willing to "tip" the driver an extra 2 cents. So when you are "doing" Italy and get used to the custom, you do not mind carrying a pound or so of copper coins and distributing them whenever you speak to a native.

The effect of this custom on the people must be very pernicious. And it takes away the charm of recognizing courtesy and hospitality as a national trait when you remember that you pay for it and it is cheap.

I wrote from Paris that the government of France has the monopoly of the tobacco business. In Italy the government has the monopoly of tobacco and salt, the two great necessities. It looks funny to go along the street and see the little government shops with the sign in Italian, "Tobacco and Salt." The Italian government doesn't sell good tobacco or good salt. The best cigars are from the island of Luzon, manufactured into alleged cigars in the government factories in Italy. The salt is heavy and coarse, something like old-style yellow-brown sugar. If you don't like the tobacco or the salt you can go without, for the government allows no competitor who might do better.

I have learned a little Italian, not so much but I can forget it when I cross the line. And that leads me to tell of a little experience with a moral. I had been so annoyed by the numerous beggars and vendors of trinkets that I asked a hotel porter who knew some English what I should say in Italian to tell them to go away. He told me something that sounded like "Muffa tora." Accordingly I went around for a couple of days saying "Muffa tora" to all that bothered me. Then a friend who knew a little more Italian happened to hear me and suggested that my language was too strong. The words were about what in America is meant by "Go-to-hell." And there I had been going around St. Peter's, St. Paul, and all the churches and art galleries in Rome, saying to half the people who approached me, "Go-to-hell," "Go-to-hell." A little knowledge is a dangerous thing.

Of course Americans stop at the best hotels, and they are about the same everywhere, being based on the French model. They are from one-third to one-half cheaper than the best hotels in American cities. We are supposed to get three meals a day: First, rolls and coffee; second, about 12 o'clock, what is really a late breakfast but is called "dejeuner" and has three to five courses: eggs (always—generally omelet), macaroni, a cutlet or chop with potatoes, a roast meat, cheese, and fruit. No coffee or tea or anything to drink except water, which they say is bad and unhealthful. Dinner at 7 o'clock and a good meal: Soup, fish, cutlet or chop with macaroni, roast, vegetables, roast chicken and salad, cheese, small cakes, and fruit. No coffee or tea. If you want coffee after dinner you have it served in the lounging-room or out-of-doors, and it is extra. Nobody but Americans drink water, and they do not use enough to hurt. When you enter the hotel you are received by the "hall porter," really the manager, who bows and takes you or sends you to a room. After a while he sends up for your name and nationality, but that is for the police. There is no hotel register. When you pay your bill and are leaving the porter rings a bell and everybody from proprietor to chambermaid appears to say "good-by," speed the parting guest and receive the parting tips. At first your royal reception and leave-taking makes quite an impression and you feel "set up," but after a while it gets to be a bore and you try to escape it but can't. The cooking and service are first-class, better than in America. There is one kind of dishes I steer clear of, those labeled on the bill of fare, "a la Americaine." They are like those served in Hutchinson, "a la Italia," or "a la Français," which means that they are probably spoiled by the cook trying to do something he does not understand.

Of course in the small Italian hotels the cooking is different, but they tell me it is good. The restaurants where the poorer people eat are full of garlicky smells which can be heard for a block. The staple articles of food for Italians are soup, macaroni and vegetables, all flavored with garlic. The ordinary Italian does not eat meat. There are probably several reasons why, but the first one is that he has not the price, and that is enough. When a man is working for 30 cents a day he is a stranger to roast beef, for meat is as high as it is in America.

I haven't seen a real clothing store in Italy. There are two classes of Italians only: The rich, who have a tailor, and the poor, who put the goods together themselves. Again I want to repeat what I have said before: The things that are cheap in Europe are those in which labor is the principal factor. When it comes to hiring a man to do work, you name your price. That is why carriage-driving, servants, clothes-making, the building trades and labor of every kind from lace-makers to railroad engineers, are so low.

The Italian shopkeepers have a well-deserved reputation as bargainers. Go into a shop, ask a price, and very likely the proprietor or clerk will say "So much: what will you give?" Americans have a reputation of being "easy," and so they usually start us with a price of "6 francs," when they will come down to one or two rather than lose a sale. When you get through you never know just how much you have been beaten—you only know you have been. Some stores advertise "fixed prices," but they are unfixed if necessary. The process of "shopping" thus has another and delicious feature for the American "shopper."

I have found the Italians honest. We hardly ever lock our room. I am always leaving the umbrella, but somebody always finds it and brings it to me, and I can't say that much for Americans. The hackmen do not overcharge, or at least not near as much as in Chicago or New York. I think a stranger is better treated in Rome than in Kansas City. But then comes the suspicious thought—we pay for it.

Previous to this trip I had often heard people talk about the fleas in Italy, and had thought it was very funny. It is no joke. At first I was much amused when I would see a well-dressed lady stop suddenly on the street, elevate her skirt and go hunting. I now consider it a perfectly justifiable and proper action. If there is a game law in Italy with a closed season on fleas it is not at this time of the year. I have seen the anxious, heart-stricken look on the faces of the martyrs and saints as painted by the old masters, and I know now where they got their models, for I have seen the man and the woman conscious of the march of the flea along the small of the back or in some other unreachable place, and have seen the haunted, hunted look on the face as conjecture what the flea would do next changed into realization. The Italian flea works a good deal like the American mosquito, only he makes no music and you can only tell where he is by sad experience. He can dodge better than some politicians and he can get in his work early and often. I am growing accustomed to the sensation myself, but I do not think I shall ever enjoy it. The Bible says the wicked flee when no man pursueth, but in Italy the wicked flea is improving each minute whether anyone pursueth or not. Mingled with art and old masters, lagoons, and gondolas, cathedrals and Cæsars, blue sky and green fields, will always be my recollection of the flea that never takes a siesta and to whom the poets have never done justice.

SWITZERLAND.

ACROSS THE ALPS.

BRIEG, SWITZERLAND, July 7, 1905.

"Beyond the Alps lies Italy" with all of its art and history and fleas. After a day on Lake Lugano and Lake Maggiore, where the two countries of Italy and Switzerland meet, and where the customs officers examined our baggage three times in the course of a trip around the water, we crossed the Alps, among which we had been for two days, and are now in the oldest republic on earth, Switzerland. We came over the Simplon Pass in a stage-coach and not through a tunnel, as we could have done. The Simplon Pass is historic and picturesque. As soon as the tunnel is completed, which has been seven years in building, the railroad train will rush through the mountains and the stage-coach will be an old fogy luxury. But the way to go over the Alps for pleasure and observation is not to take a tunnel train, but ride over on the outside of a coach with five horses and see the panorama as you pass by. After a fortnight spent among the great works of man, cathedrals, coliseums and galleries, one day was enough in the Simplon to prove that Nature is still ahead. The great amphitheatres of the mountains, the magnificent stage-settings of forest and peak, left the coliseum and the forum far behind. The changing hues of the slopes, now gradual and now precipitate, sometimes bare and sometimes covered with pasture and vineyard or forest, were in colors which even the old masters could not equal. It was an all-day drive over a fine road, through narrow gulches, alongside rushing rivers, under waterfalls of melted snow, finally through the snow itself, and then down, almost sliding, with the coach-wheels locked so they were like runners, into the quaint little town of Brieg.

The road over the Simplon was built by Napoleon. All over the map of Europe you will see such monuments to the name of the great emperor. I do not give Napoleon much credit for the job, as it was a military necessity to him. He had to keep an army in Italy and always be on the lookout for his enemies there, so he ordered the

Simplon Pass, up to the time only a trail, to be provided with a macadamized road, and it was done. I have seen so many of such roads in Europe that I would be willing to support Napoleon for road overseer or street commissioner any time. The road was completed in 1807, and the tunnel under the Pass will be finished in 1906. It is sixteen miles long, large enough for a double track, and has been constructed from both ends at the same time. To my mind it is a great engineering feat to start two small holes in a mountain, sixteen miles apart, and figure so accurately that those holes will meet some place in the center over a mile from the daylight on top. I suppose it looks easy to the engineer who knows how, but it is miraculous to me. A good many lives have been lost and a lot of money spent on this tunnel, but those are the sacrifices the world demands before it will move on.

The road over the Pass is forty-five miles long. Soon after starting, all agriculture disappeared, except vineyards and pasture. The vineyards continued almost up to the snow. Wherever there was enough ground there were vines, and in many places the mountain-side was terraced and in the made land the vines were growing profusely. Literally speaking, there are mountains of vineyards in northern Italy and in Switzerland.

Cattle-raising in the Alps is done in small herds and is mostly on the Swiss side. The stock looks smooth and fine. Along with a drove of cows are always a few goats. In the early summer the herdsmen drive the animals up the paths and trails to the little patches of rich pasture, where they feed until fall, neither man nor beast coming down until driven by the cold. I saw cattle pasturing on the mountain-side where it was so steep it seemed they must have feet like flies or they would tumble down. Of course the animals inherit the mountain knowledge, and I suppose they don't know there is such a thing as a level meadow. Here and there men and women would be cutting grass with a scythe, spreading the hay out to dry, and then actually rolling it down the mountain-side. Like all people who live in mountainous countries, the Swiss herdsmen along the Simplon looked intelligent, cheerful and poor.

And that brings me to another broken idol. I had always heard of a Swiss "chalet," and had supposed it was an artistic, smart-looking house perched up on a peak for everybody to see. A real Swiss chalet is a half dugout in a valley, built of stone and whitewashed once, in which the family lives upstairs and the cattle spend the winter in the basement, never going out until the springtime comes. Now I can see the economy, the advantages and the necessity of a Swiss "chalet," but I can't see anything beautiful or poetic, for such qualities are not present. I had the same experience with an Italian "villa," which I found by observation was usually a plain-appearing stone house built around a court, inhabited by Italians, goats and chickens, and principally remembered by the noisome odor.

I have done some touring in the Rocky Mountains, and I was curious to see what difference there would be between the Rockies and the Alps,—both having peaks of about the same height, and each forming the backbone of a continent. The Alps have more snow than the Rockies. All of the peaks are snow-covered and the gulches of snow run far down the mountain-side here in July. Only an occasional peak in Colorado has snow, and then only a little, not enough to call it "snow-covered." To my mind the Rockies are more grandly picturesque. The sides of the Alps are cultivated and covered with vines, dotted with pasture and cattle nearly up to the timber-line. The Rockies are still as nature left them, more stern and desolate, awe-inspiring and effective. The Alps do not look like the Rockies, except in height and steepness. The foliage of the trees is not the same, and the Alps have a tamer appearance than the American range. A town in the Rockies is out of harmony with the scenery. A village in the Alps adds to the beauty. Perhaps I do not make myself clear, but there is a great difference, and I think the Rockies are far ahead from a mountain standpoint.

Switzerland has no language of its own. The Swiss have four distinct languages, and the people of one part of the country do not understand the other. In some of the cantons (corresponding to our states) the language is French, in some German, in some Italian, and in some a composite speech based on the Latin and called "the Romance language." Remember, this is a country of about the same area (15,000 miles) as the Seventh Congressional district of Kansas, but also remember it is cut up by the mountains into natural divisions which are hard to overcome. I am getting used to hearing one language in one town and another in the next across an imaginary line. But four kinds of talk within a little country like Switzerland is going to be hard to contend with.

Right at the top of the Simplon Pass among the snows that never entirely melt is a "hospice," maintained for generations by an order of monks and devoted to taking care of poor travelers or relieving those in distress or who lose their way. On every pass between Switzerland and Italy there is such a hospice. The monks have the great St. Bernard dogs (named from the St. Bernard Pass, a little distance away), and when the snows get deep the dogs do much of the work of rescue. I had heard of these great institutions since boyhood, and wondered if they would turn out badly when actually seen. But they are all right, and their good work has not been exaggerated in the thrilling stories in which they have figured.

There are many very large and very picturesque waterfalls, many more than in the Rockies. The constantly melting snow keeps them running, and it is not uncommon to see the water tumbling or jumping down a sheer descent of two hundred to five hundred feet. I would like to take a few waterfalls of that kind back to Kansas and put them up in the sand-hills. I offered an Italian gentleman on the coach who spoke some English to trade him 160 acres of western Kansas land for a good first-class waterfall. Almost fifteen minutes after I made the proposition he laughed. It doesn't do any good to be funny with people who don't know your language.

GENEVA AND CHILLON.

GENEVA, July 9, 1905.

This little city, now containing nearly 100,000 inhabitants, has been a storm-center in Europe for 2000 years. Cæsar mentions it, and during the early centuries when Rome was conquering and governing most of the known world, Geneva was an important place, both from a strategic standpoint as a gate to Helvetia and as a prosperous and loyal town. It was either the capital of the country or a ruling city during all of the Dark and Medieval ages, and was one of the first where people learned popular sovereignty and applied it to the detriment of the reigning king or duke. By playing one side against another in the struggle for sovereignty the popular leaders fought for freedom of conscience, and about the year 1500 secured practical independence. Then the Reformation commenced, and Calvin fled from Paris to Geneva. The people there were naturally "agin the government," and they took up Calvin's doctrine, and during the years of fighting over religion Geneva was the center from which Protestantism drew most of its leadership and inspiration. They fought for freedom of conscience and worship, and if anybody disagreed with them they killed him promptly to convince him of his error. Calvin ruled Geneva during his life, and after his death his cause went marching on. During the last century Geneva has made a reputation for manufacturing watches, jewelry and musical instruments. It is only fair to say that the best Geneva watches are now made in America. The work here is nearly all done by hand in the home of the workman, and the watchmakers of Geneva have had a hard time competing with Yankee machinery and ingenuity.

The surroundings of Geneva are peaceful and beautiful. The big lake of blue water comes to an end at the Geneva quay and rushes out into the world as the river Rhone, clear and sparkling. Mont Blanc, a quiet old stager of a mountain, whose head is always covered with snow, looks over the city like a stately sentinel at his post. Mountains rise all around the lake and are covered with vineyards, almost the only product of the soil, stretching far up the heights connecting the blue of the lake with the blue of the sky and the snowy peaks and white clouds which watch over them. Amid such surroundings we had decided to rest a few days from our travel, and I found it the best place in the world just to sit in the hotel garden from which the lake, Mont Blanc and the entire picture are visible, and just loaf and loaf and loaf.

THE ALPINE HUNTER OF TO-DAY

The great amusement of tourists who come to Switzerland is mountain-climbing. I have learned the game. Men and women come in at night recounting the wonderful feats they have accomplished and the dangers they have escaped. Everybody carries an "alpenstock," which is a sharp-pointed cane with a chamois handle, and whenever he climbs a peak he has a ring burned around the stick, and shows it as proudly as the Indian once did the notches which meant deaths of enemies. I am a little skeptical, and listen to the climbing stories as I do to fish stories at home. It is too much like golf where you keep your own count. Perhaps I shall yield to the demands of environment enough to get me an alpenstock and have a few rings burned in it so I can have a few chips in the game, as it were. The men run to knickerbockers, wear feathers in their hats and carry packs on their shoulders. The women wear short skirts which don't hang well and big shoes with nails in the soles—I am speaking now of people who do the thing right, and not those who sit on the porch and loaf.

The Swiss themselves are degenerating from the simple-hearted people they were. They have fallen before the temptations of the tourists. They see the American and the Englishman with lots of money to spend, and they find it easier to separate the stranger from his cash than they do to hunt chamois and herd cattle. It is a cause of much regret to the intelligent Swiss that this is so, but I do not notice the intelligent mourners going out into the mountains and setting an example of industry. They sell the jewelry, the souvenirs, the milk and the wine at advanced prices, and they have the greatest number of hotels and boarding-houses of any country on earth. If you enjoy handsome little shops with trinkets and gewgaws, jewelry and picture cards, carved wood and imitation stones, as I do, you would thoroughly enjoy wandering through Geneva. The Geneva artisan will take a chair-leg and make a musical instrument. Sit down on a sofa and you will be startled to hear a piece of Wagner's played by the concealed music-box.

The language spoken in Geneva is French. I do not think it is good French, for the people here do not understand the French with the fine Parisian accent I brought from Paris. But a large proportion of the people understand English. I am of the opinion that in spite of the fact that French is still the international language in Europe, the one you can use with educated people nearly anywhere, the English-American is the coming language. Very few people in Europe travel. The Germans do so more than others, but the French seldom do, the Italians rarely, and the Spanish and the Russians practically never. The English come to the continent in great numbers, and the Americans are in droves. In a place like Geneva in the principal shops and on the promenades you would say that fully half the people were English-speaking. In order to take care of these profitable guests the Swiss and others are learning enough of the language to sell them cheap goods at high prices, and they will learn more. It is not an uncommon experience to go into a store and after laboriously constructing a question in alleged French to get an answer in very fair English.

I am told that up to a few years ago the American traveler was regarded with a little contempt by the people of continental Europe, and considered as only so much soil from which to gather wealth. But Americans of experience tell me that since the war with Spain all this has changed. As for myself, these Europeans have always spoken in the friendliest way of America, even when they did not know there were any Yankees around. The theory that we were only a commercial people and would not fight (the world loves a fighter) was disproven so thoroughly that they have rather gone to the other extreme, and Americans are now very popular as Americans and not merely for their money. Europe also has the highest opinion of McKinley and Roosevelt. With a great deal of pride in my heart I read a leading editorial in the London Times saying that Roosevelt's letter to Russia and Japan urging peace was one of the greatest of state papers. The Times added that it was "straightforward, frank and clear—the American idea of diplomacy." All of Europe now regards America as a great and friendly power, and an American swells up considerably more over his country when he is in other nations than he does at home, where he is apt to get fussy and cynical. The English are not popular on the continent, though England is feared and respected. The Americans are liked because they are believed to be fair and square.

At the other end of Lake Geneva is the castle of Chillon. It is about as big as the court-house in Hutchinson, and looks like the old sugar-mill, only more so. Byron did a great deal for the people in that neck of the woods, for his poem made the castle famous, and tourists come by the hundreds and buy. In return they have named the big hotel the Byron, which shows they are not ungrateful. Byron's poem had the poor prisoner confined in a dungeon with two brothers, and he had the torture of seeing them die. The facts are that there never was any "prisoner of Chillon" except in the brilliant imagination of Lord Byron. Of course many prisoners were confined in the dungeon. Every castle in Europe has a dungeon, and none of them were constructed with an idea of sanitary conditions or the health of the prisoners. But the dungeon at Chillon is the lightest and airiest dungeon I have seen. It is as comfortable as a good many hotel rooms in the United States. The only prisoner of note that had any such experience was a preacher named Bonnivard, who was kept there for two years because he believed or didn't believe in Calvin,—I have forgotten which it was. Bonnivard had no brothers, and lived a number of years afterward and said he enjoyed his confinement at Chillon because he had so much time to think. Our guide showed our party the pathway the prisoner's feet had worn in the rock where he had walked back and forth within the limit of his chains. I couldn't see the path, although everybody else did. The rest of the castle of Chillon is very interesting, as it was the residence of a fine line of dukes who were always fighting either for or against the king. Our guide, who spoke only French, told us all about it, but I shall not repeat what she said. The people of Hutchinson would not understand her remarks any better than I did.

My idea of a good joke is to have a guide who can only talk French tell an American who can't understand French something very important or serious. The Frenchman tells his story with rapidity, earnestness and gestures. The American listens with frank impatience and punctuates the French sentences with American ejaculations which have no connection with the subject. The Frenchman acts mad, but he isn't at all. The American acts pleasant, but he is really mad.

The castle of Chillon is in the lake, about sixty feet from the shore. You reach the entrance over a bridge after fighting your way through the sellers of souvenirs. That is one thing the old dukes did not have to contend with. If they were still doing business I think they would fill up the dungeon with the salesmen and salesladies.

SOMETHING OF SWITZERLAND.

ZURICH, SWITZERLAND, July 12, 1905.

Switzerland is a succession of beautiful lakes, mountains and big hotels, dotted here and there with manufacturing towns and vineyards. It has been said that you cannot get too much of a good thing, but that is a mistake. Even the man who loves pie must admit that after he has had all the pie he can consume three times a day for a week, he would want to change the subject. After one has been traveling through Swiss scenery for seven days he is almost satisfied. We no longer chase across the car to see a big mountain-peak, or hurry out of the hotel soon after our arrival to behold the lake. And men and women with feathers in their hats and alpenstocks in their hands do not make us turn our heads. The sight of a little level country would look mighty good, and a comfortable seat on the porch comes nearer to filling the longing in my heart than the sight of a waterfall or an old castle several minutes' walk distant.

Lucerne is the center of the tourist travel. All roads into Switzerland lead to Lucerne, and the scenery is more varied than at any other of the show places. The town is on the lake and the mountains are around it. From my hotel I could see Mount Pilatus, the place where they say Pontius Pilate finally found a resting-place. At the other end of the view is the snow-covered Rigi, and there are all kinds of Alps in the background. Lucerne looks like an American summer resort. It is made up of hotels and souvenir shops, and elegantly dressed women parade up and down the promenade walks, while rich old gentlemen sit uncomfortably around the piazzas and wish the women-folks had let them stay at home. It is astonishing how many men act as if they would give a good deal to be at work somewhere rather than in Switzerland "enjoying themselves." A lot of people do not know how to have a good time or how to see a strange and delightful place. I meet many people who do not care for Europe, or Italy, or Switzerland,— the people who bring a stack of trunks and good clothes and have to put in their time dressing up only to be out-dressed by somebody else.

But Lucerne has one thing different. It is the "Lion of Lucerne," the monument erected in honor of the Swiss soldiers who died in the French palace defending the rotten Bourbon dynasty when the revolutionists broke in and captured the king and queen. The lion (twenty-eight feet in length) is carved out of a sandstone ledge, and is the finest monument or statue I ever saw. The king of beasts is dying, agony on his face, a broken lance in his side, and his huge paw resting on a shield of the lilies of France. The more I looked at the great work of Thorwaldsen the more I felt it, and I went back again and again to see it,—the real test of effect. Nearly everyone has seen copies or pictures of this work, but it is one of the things that no copy can do justice to, for the size and substance of the stone, the pathos and power of the subject and the skill and the genius of the sculptor have met most perfectly and impressively.

Near Lucerne is the scene of the early struggle for Swiss liberty. Around the lake of Lucerne are the three cantons of Uri, Schwyz, and Unterwalden, whose representatives met some 500 years ago and entered into the compact to stand together for freedom, a compact which has never been broken. Here William Tell refused to take off his hat to the hat the tyrant Gessler had set up and ordered all to salute. To punish Tell the governor ordered him to take his bow and arrow and shoot an apple from the head of his son. Tell's aim was true, but as he turned away another arrow dropped from his coat. When asked why he had that, he said it was for Gessler if the boy had been hurt. Gessler took Tell in a boat and was carrying him to a dungeon, when a storm arose and Tell was released in order to use his skill as a boatman. He knew that the world wasn't big enough for both himself and Gessler, so he soon after inserted an arrow into the tyrant's ribs, and the Austrians had to get a new governor.

Some cynical historians doubt this Tell story, but I do not. It is just as good a story as a lot which appear in history and it is good enough to be true.

After the Tell revolution, which was in the thirteenth century, those Swiss cantons never lost their freedom, although they had to fight for it about every generation. The Hapsburg family, which reigned in Austria, was always trying to conquer the Swiss, and although its power was great enough to overcome any army they could collect, it could not cope with the mountains and gulches in which the Swiss were at home, and where one man who knew the land was equal in fighting value to a dozen knights in armor or on horseback. On that account the Swiss, especially the people of these "forest cantons," have been a free people through all the changes in the world during more than 500 years. Sometimes they have been selfish and narrow in their ideas of freedom, considering that they were the only people on earth, and they have until the last century held serfs and domineered despotically over weak neighbors. But they were always far in advance of the rest of the world in their ideas of personal liberty. Switzerland is the one country which has always been a refuge to exiled patriots, rebels, conspirators and pretenders. Switzerland will not surrender a fugitive from another country on a political charge. The judges who sentenced Charles I. of England to death sought refuge in Switzerland when Charles II. came to the throne. Charles demanded that the judges be given up to him, and brought every influence to bear, but the Swiss stood by their law of refuge. To-day the anarchists and nihilists of Russia and the revolutionists of every country from Roumania to Spain have their headquarters in Geneva or some other Swiss town.

It will be noticed that I think a good deal of the Swiss, and that I have written some criticism of the Italians. I went through Italy without ever being overcharged, "held up," or worked by cab-drivers, hotel-keepers, or anyone at all. But in Switzerland, the land of freedom and education, I have had all these things done to me. I have been surprised and pleased by the way the people of Europe treat strangers, even if they do want tips. I had not been meanly treated from the time I left Boston until I reached Switzerland. The last man I did business with in my native land was a Boston hackman, who charged me twice what he should when he brought us to the ship. I did not meet his equal until I got to Lucerne. I hope there is no connection between personal liberty, republican government, and the swindling of strangers.

Yesterday we went to St. Gallen, a little industrial town near Constance. The women will recognize the name of this town if the men do not, for it is the place Swiss embroideries come from. I found out one thing there: Most of the Swiss hand embroidery is made by machinery. The Swiss are called the Yankees of Europe. They are up to almost all the tricks of the trade. They are changing from a pastoral and agricultural people, except right in the mountains, and are making money out of manufactories and tourists. The men and women do not wear the ridiculous and charming peasant costumes, except in beer-gardens and summer-resort hotels. In fact, I am impressed with the sameness of people's clothes everywhere. There is no longer any such thing as characteristic costume. I saw the men's clothes in Italy all cut and made just as in France, England, or America. The women have the same styles in the country districts of Switzerland that they do in Kansas or in Paris. Of course some people know how to wear their clothes better than others, and there is a difference in fit and make, but the styles are the same from Hutchinson to St. Gallen.

I am learning some things in geography. Mont Blanc, the biggest mountain in Switzerland, is in France. Constance, one of the best Swiss resorts, is in Germany. Switzerland is such a busy little country that it bulges out all around.

SWISS AND SWITZERLAND.

NEUHAUSEN, SWITZERLAND, July 13, 1905.

Soon after I arrived in Switzerland I inquired at a Geneva hotel the name of the President of the Republic of Switzerland. The hall porter (about the same as chief clerk) could not tell me, nor could he find out on inquiry around the office. Several times in Geneva I asked the same question, but always in vain. One or two men thought they knew, but they were not sure, and, as I learned afterward, they guessed wrong. I kept at the work of finding out who was the chief executive until I reached Lucerne. In a bookstore there my question aroused the interest of the proprietor, who spoke good English, and he inquired around until he found out that the President of Switzerland is named Brenner. During the process I suppose I asked a dozen educated Swiss, and three-fourths of them could give me promptly the name of the President of the United States, but not the name of their own President. Of course there is a reason for what would be fearful ignorance in any other country. The President of Switzerland doesn't amount to as much as the Vice-President of the United States, and it would stagger a good many Americans to tell who was Vice-President before Roosevelt. Switzerland is a rather loosely bound together confederation of cantons (states). The cantons are jealous of the federal government, and give it very little power. Up to a few years ago there would be tariffs in some cantons against importations from others. The general government has the power to do the international business, but Switzerland keeps out of European politics. It would have little or no power as an offensive nation with its three million of people, and so it contents itself with furnishing scenery, wine, watches, music-boxes and good air to the inhabitants of other countries who are able to buy. The federal government consists of a congress composed of representatives from the cantons made up like our Senate and House. This congress elects an executive committee of seven, and the President of Switzerland is merely the chairman of that executive committee. Berne is the capital of Switzerland and the congress meets there, but it can only propose important legislation, which is then submitted to the people, who usually defeat it. The cantons of Switzerland have various kinds of republican government. Some have legislatures, some councils, and in a few of the small ones, where it is practicable, the government acts by mass meetings of the people, with an executive or a committee to carry out the legislation. The small area of the country and of the twenty-two cantons (they average about the size of Reno county, but some are not bigger than a commissioner district) makes the government a peculiar proposition. There is no foreign immigration, no uneducated class, and no one whose ancestors have not been self-governing for a generation. And yet as they have remodeled their local and federal constitutions and charters, they have come closer to the American methods all the time, the only important difference being the initiative and referendum, which is after all only a continuance of their ancient "land gemeinde," or mass meetings of the people at which measures were considered and officers elected, the voting now being done by ballot instead of holding up the hands.

As I have written before, in some cantons the people use one language and in some another. Likewise in some everybody is a Protestant and in others everybody is a Catholic; very seldom both faiths in one canton. During the Reformation and for a number of years afterward the Swiss fought and killed each other for the love of God as fiercely as in any other country. Switzerland and southern Germany, which borders on it, were the fields in which the great Reformers did their best and worst work. The Reformation in Switzerland was double-headed. One branch, led by Calvin, was marked by what we call Puritan austerity, and had its headquarters at Geneva. From there went John Knox to Scotland and a host of eminent preachers to England and other countries, forming what is now called the Presbyterian Church. Zwingli, at Zurich, was a milder, gentler teacher, and his kind of Protestantism grew most in Switzerland. Luther, only a little way off, had still another kind of Protestantism, and each of the three differed considerably in confession of faith, Calvin standing on the principle of predestination, Luther holding to transubstantiation, or the doctrine of the actual presence of the body of our Saviour in communion, Zwingli insisting that communion was only symbolic. Mutual friends brought Zwingli and Luther together, and when they could not agree, Zwingli held out his hand in parting and Luther would not even shake hands. Zwingli was killed in a battle in a religious war with the Catholics, but his creed really became the dominant one in

Swiss Protestantism. Calvin had Servetus burned to death because he denied the trinity.

So you see in the good old days in Switzerland there was a hard time for the plain and honest person trying to do what was right. Those times are past now, and Protestant and Catholic cantons get along peaceably; but there is still friction. Each canton in Switzerland looks after its educational matters and there are good schools everywhere. In nearly every city is a big university. I suppose that in proportion to population there are more university graduates in Switzerland than in any other country on earth. In America the young men and women too often cut short their education in order to get into business. In Switzerland, there are no such alluring opportunities, and the students stay till graduation. A young Swiss will go through the university and then go to work at the trade of his father. In America the young man would want to "do better" and really does worse by becoming a lawyer or an editor. Even good things have their bad features, and American colleges make mighty poor professional men out of material which was intended for good mechanics and farmers.

We spent a couple of days in Zurich, the largest city of Switzerland. Its special industry is silk-making, and the silk and embroidery stores are beautiful. The main business street of Zurich has two rows of trees like First avenue in Hutchinson, and the result is a delightful change from the usual hot, bare main street of a city. And that reminds me that it is a law in Switzerland or in the forest cantons that no one can cut down a tree except by official permission, and then another must be planted to take its place.

In the agricultural and pastoral parts of Switzerland a great deal of land is held "in common," that is government land, under the control of the canton, not for sale at any price, but for the use of the people of the community under strict regulations. So a Swiss peasant will have a few acres of land of his own, a few cattle, and a right as a citizen to pasture on the common ground and a share of the profits of the forest. Immigration is not invited, although tourists with money are welcomed, for the more people the less the share of each in the common fund. There can hardly be any poverty in Switzerland, except, of course, in the cities. Every Swiss peasant can make a living if he will work. But neither can he be expected to get rich nor be a bigger man than his father. He must follow the beaten path marked out by centuries of custom and more firmly established than the unwritten constitution of the country.

I am getting more and more impressed with the fallacy of "cheapness" in Europe. Comparing prices with those of Hutchinson, I find that the things which are cheaper here are silks, kid gloves, diamonds, and the products of labor like embroidery, lace, clocks, wood carvings, tailor-made clothes and straw hats (poorly made). Cotton goods, linen goods, shoes, iron and steel, bread and meat, coffee, and most of what we call necessities of life, are higher in Europe than in America. It is the people who are cheap and not the things; and when I say "cheap" I do not mean lacking in energy, ability, or industry, but in opportunity to make more than a living, to have leisure or the common luxuries and often necessities.

This is the last night in Switzerland. To-morrow we cross the line to Constance, which is in Germany, and which is spelled Konstanz and abbreviated "Kaz.," which makes it near to "Kas." Neuhausen is the place where the Rhine makes its big leap down the rocks, a fall of sixty feet, and on account of the volume of water the grandest in Europe. It is the Niagara Falls of the Alpine country, but it is not in the same class with Niagara Falls, U. S. A. The Rhine is about as wide as the Kaw at Topeka, but much deeper, and the falls are about four times the height of Bowersock's dam at Lawrence. A beautiful hotel faces the roaring torrent as it precipitates itself over the rocks amid clouds of spray. The prices at the hotel are higher than the falls. I can only call to mind one place where you feel that you are being more genteelly robbed with your own consent, and that is at Niagara Falls, New York. But our Niagara Falls are higher to correspond.

GERMANY.

IN THE BLACK FOREST.

TRIBERG, GERMANY, July 17, 1905.

 This is a small town in the middle of the Black Forest. I had read a good deal of the Black Forest, but really had no idea what it was. The name sounded as if it might be a part of Arkansas or Louisiana, and I think I was looking for swamps and waste land covered with underbrush and impenetrable to travelers except on made roads. But as a matter of fact it is as delightful and beautiful a country as I have seen since I left Kansas. The land is mountainous, but it is fertile and the valleys and hillsides are dotted with thrifty-looking little farms. The name applies, all right, for the mountains are covered with dense forests of spruce trees with a dark-green foliage which looks really black. The farming land has evidently been cleared in the centuries that have passed since the roving Germans settled into peaceful peasants and quit their occupation of making Rome howl by raiding and pillaging the towns of the declining empire. The Black Forest covers a great part of southwest Germany, mostly in the state or grand duchy of Baden. Up to a short time ago it had a number of practically independent little kingdoms about the size of your hat, which were in a perpetual struggle for existence and recognition. Anthony Hope used the Black Forest as the scene for his Zenda stories, and to-day we came through the principality of Fürstenberg, one of his favorite places, in which the prince of Fürstenberg still holds an honorary position but under the actual government of Emperor William. I also noticed that the prince was proprietor of a big brewery.

 It is harvest-time in the Black Forest, and men and women are gathering the crops, small grain and hay, using the hand-sickle and the hand-rake but doing their work in a thorough manner. When they get through the raking I don't suppose there is a waste straw left lying on the ground or a kernel of grain which is not carefully picked up. The farmer in Europe would get rich on what an American farmer drops on the way from the field to the barn. They have fine horses and cattle in the Black Forest, and look prosperous. When one horse is used in a wagon he is harnessed alongside the pole and not between shafts. I was told the reason was that it was to make it easy to add another horse if desired without changing the pole. That was nearly as strange as the one horse alongside the pole.

The time is past when the sight of ladies working in the field excites any interest, although I still have a little feeling when the woman is sixty or seventy years old. It is not so bad in Germany, and especially in the Black Forest, where the air is light and exhilarating; and then the men work too. In Italy the hauling was done by animals as follows: Horses, oxen, cows, dogs, women. Sometimes a woman and a dog were hitched together to small wagons, especially milk carts. In Switzerland the dogs were still in harness, but the women were out of it. And in the Black Forest I believe the dogs are freed, as all the vehicles I have seen have been drawn by horses or oxen. Perhaps it will be different later. I write now only of the Black Forest. We drove for twelve miles down one of the valleys and through the little villages. A number of the old peasant costumes were worn by women and girls, although most of them were dressed in the same styles as in Paris or Hutchinson. A very striking head-dress for the feminine is one of the Black Forest styles, a bonnet with two large wings extending upward at an angle of about 40 degrees from the head, and with flowing bands several feet long down the back. Girls and unmarried women have bright-colored wings and bands, married women must wear black. By the way, the women of continental Europe wherever we have been have worn earrings,—France, Italy, and Switzerland. As American women generally discarded these disfiguring ornaments several years ago, the sight has been a strange one. Especially in Italy are the earrings large and imposing, rich and poor vieing with each other in size of the pendants and rings.

Aside from agriculture the main industry of the Black Forest is wood-carving and clock-making. There are some small factories, but as a rule the work is done at home; and it is very good. We visited one of these home shops, and the whole family showed us their handiwork. A beautifully carved wooden hall clock with a cuckoo and a music-box which played every half-hour was only $4

American money. It must have taken the man a week to make it, and in our country the price would have been several times as large. There is a big tariff on this ware going into America, and it is all right. If it were not so, our American wood-workers would have to learn another trade or work for $4 or $5 a week. And if they got only $4 or $5 a week they would not eat much meat, buy much clothing, or pay for many newspapers. See?

The people of the Black Forest are a charming, friendly lot. I suppose they are as happy as anybody, although one of them was very proud of a brother who had gone to America and was making "much geld," and whom he would follow if he could. All through Europe I meet people who have relatives in America, and that may account for the friendly treatment I have everywhere received. These American relatives have all gotten "rich" according to their European relatives, which shows that the immigrants to our country all succeed or keep a stiff upper lip when they write to the folks in the fatherland.

The architecture of the Black Forest houses is as striking as any I have seen. Nearly every farmhouse is very large, at least three stories high, and on one or more sides the roof "gambrels" off from the high ridge nearly to the ground. The effect is like a tent-covering, and the roof is often thatched or tiled in two or three colors,—on some the green grass is growing. Part of the house is the barn. The winter here is said to be severe, and the Forest peasant evidently believes in having his family and his horses, cows and chickens where they can be comfortable and sociable. The houses are extra clean, and the furniture, dishes and utensils of the kitchen shine with the good polishing they must receive. The little farms are tilled to the limit, and are generally irrigated and always fertilized. Just to show how these people manage to get a living out of the ground and the care they use to get it all, I saw women and men on the roadside with baskets cleaning the road of manure and carrying it to their land.

We have had to learn a new money system in Germany. France, Italy, Switzerland and Belgium have what is called a "Latin league,"

with interchangeable currency, the unit being the franc (France, Switzerland, and Belgium), and the lire (Italy). But Germany joins no Latin leagues. The unit of the German currency is the "mark," equivalent to twenty-five cents American. This is divided into one hundred pfennigs. Prices are carried out to the pfennig, and one-pfennig coins (in value one-fourth of one cent) are seen more than our one-cent pieces at home. That illustrates the close, exact, economical German spirit. The first time I made a small purchase in Germany I got a pocketful of change. Mrs. Morgan wanted a little money, and I gave her a couple of handfuls. She said she didn't want so much, as she only intended to buy inexpensive things. I had actually given her about fifty cents. When one hundred copper coins make twenty-five cents and they are used in most transactions, you can realize what a heavy load you carry and how you can get that wealthy feeling without much actual expense.

Soon after leaving Constance our road turned away from the Rhine, and going through a tunnel we were in the valley of the Danube. It startled me a little, as I had always connected the Danube with Austria and Turkey. But sure enough, we were riding along the banks of the Danube, which has been made famous by history, poetry and music. If a raindrop fell on one side of that hill it would go down to the Rhine to the Baltic, and if the wind blew it over to the other side before it struck the earth it would start eastward and journey down the Danube to the Black sea. Rivers are like human beings,—they get their directions from the place where they start and go onward along the road of least resistance to the place appointed, unless dammed or taken up by man or God, in which case they will struggle and work to seep back to the channel in which it was intended they should make their course.

By the way, the "Beautiful Blue Danube" is not blue at all in this part of its career, but almost black, seemingly taking its hue from the forests in which it has its origin.

The town of Triberg is a quaint little place near the top of the mountain, and apparently about one hundred miles from Nowhere. I have had my first experience with what I understand is not infrequent in old German towns. There is a tax on strangers, thirty pfennigs a day or one mark a week, and our hotel has to pay and charge in our bill. Ministers of the gospel, and paupers, are exempt. In America if they had a fool tax like that they would also exempt newspaper men. The only way I could get out of paying the tax was to make affidavit that I was a minister or a pauper, so I reluctantly gave up the offer to dodge taxation and the town of Triberg is fifteen cents to the good on account of our stay. However, there is a very fine waterfall, and we looked fifteen cents' worth at that and called it even.

STORIES OF STRASSBURG.

STRASSBURG, GERMANY, July 18, 1905.

To use the American vernacular, Strassburg is a good town. It has the best-looking stores, the most energetic acting people and the most thriving appearance of any city since we left Paris. The reason for this is probably the mingling of the German and the French and the location of the city as the metropolis of a very rich territory lying in both countries. Strassburg is a German city in which the people are at heart French. Thirty years ago the treaty which ended the Franco-German war gave Strassburg and two of the rich provinces of eastern France, Alsace and Lorraine, to the German empire. But it did not give the German emperor a warranty deed to the hearts of the people, and they long for their old associations. Probably the new generation is not so much disposed to France, and the influence of education and environment will gradually change the desire of the Alsatians to be sometime reunited with their old countrymen, but time and again to-day in talking with the Strassburgers they have given me to understand that they were not Germans but French.

Strassburg has a history as a city on its own account. Away back in 1300 the people revolted from the rule of the bishop who was their sovereign, and gained their independence. For 400 years Strassburg was what is known as a "free city," owing some allegiance to the German empire but governing itself and doing about as it pleased. The language, the customs and the sympathy of the people were German. In 1681 Louis XIV. of France in a time of peace seized Strassburg, and a few years later in a general treaty France was confirmed in the title, and from that time until

1871 it was a French city. During the war of 1870 Strassburg did not surrender to the overwhelming German army until its defenses were battered down and the city bombarded. And as I wrote from Paris, in the galaxy of statues representing the cities of France in the Parisian Place de la Concorde, the statue of Strassburg is hung with emblems of mourning, and some day France will fight to get the city back. Germany knows this, and the city has been strongly fortified and a garrison of 15,000 German soldiers is kept there. So many soldiers in a city of 150,000 people give a showy look to the streets, the promenades and the public places, and doubtless is a good thing financially for the merchants.

Since leaving Italy I have sworn off on cathedrals, but I had to go to the one here because it is a good one and because of the Strassburg clock. The spire of the Strassburg cathedral is one of the highest in Europe, 465 feet, beating by a few feet St. Peter's at Rome and St. Paul's in London. The rest of the building is just the ordinary cathedral except for the clock. The first big clock was constructed here in 1352 and it lasted two centuries, when another took its place, to be succeeded sixty years ago by the present one. This clock is about the size of the front of an ordinary church. It not only tells the hour and minute of the day, but the day of the week, the month of the year, the feast days of the church, and is regulated to run for centuries, automatically making the right figures for leap years and adapting itself to the revolution of feast and fast days for an almost unlimited number of years. Every fifteen minutes an angel figure strikes the bell for the quarter-hour, and figures representing boyhood, youth, manhood and old age come out for the appropriate quarters. A skeleton strikes the hour and another reverses an hour-glass. At noon there is a parade of the twelve apostles before the Saviour, and a big rooster at one side crows loudly twice before Peter gets to the front and the third time as he passes. I am getting a great sympathy for Peter because he has that story thrown up to him in so many cathedrals, churches and pictures in Europe. It seems to me that Peter did enough after that to entitle him to a rest on the cock-crow story.

Next to the cathedral clock the most interesting sight to my mind was the washerwomen's boats in the river. About 500 women were in these canal-shaped boats washing clothes, rinsing them in the river and having a good gossiping time of it. The emperor of Germany has a palace in Strassburg where he spends at least three days every year in the month of May. I did not know this, so when I saw the imperial palace on the city map I told the driver to take us there. I had never met Emperor William and he had never met me. I entered the palace door as directed by the cab-driver and was pleasantly received by a fine, portly gentleman. Of course I knew he wasn't the emperor, so I spoke in a dignified way as becomes an American citizen toying with the effete monarchies of Europe, and asked the gentleman in my best German if the emperor was at home, at the same time assuring him that if the emperor was busy not to bother him, as I could come again after supper when he would be through his work. The fat gentleman bowed and told me the emperor was here only in May, and asked me if we would like to go over the palace. I spoke up abruptly, as if I were used to running around palaces; that as I had nothing else to do just then, having laid out to put in a short time with Emperor Bill, I wouldn't mind if I did. He was a very nice man, a court chamberlain, he said, and he took Mrs. Morgan and me all through the palace and the big dining-room and ball-room and the king's den, and all that sort of thing. Before we went onto the polished floors of the big rooms we had to put felt slippers on over our shoes—a good thing to keep the floors from getting scratched, and I suppose it is a kind of ground rule that Mrs. Emperor has made to protect the varnish from the hobnailed boots of William's friends. I hope the custom won't spread to America.

The German emperor has a mighty good house in Strassburg, and it has been furnished regardless of expense. There was a notice up, "Visitors not allowed to sit on the chairs," but I wasn't very tired anyway. I looked for a sign not to spit on the floor to go with some of the other wall decoration, but it must have been overlooked. The house looked stiff, and I don't believe Bill has much fun at home and probably his wife makes him go out on the porch to smoke. I was sorry not to meet the emperor, as we will not get to Berlin, and I had some things to tell him. However, I feel that I have done the proper thing by calling on him and not waiting for him to hunt me up.

※ ※ ※

There is not so much American-made stuff in Europe as I expected. There is a good deal, but in fact these Germans and French are up to about everything that we are, and sometimes they have us bested. The Singer sewing-machine is everywhere, even in Italy. American shoes are the leaders in their lines in every city. American typewriters are sold ahead of European. Wernicke bookcases and office furniture are advertised and sold almost as at home. But the list of American goods is not very long, or else they are sold under other names and brands. To-day we bought a good picture of a typical German girl to take home with us as our art collection from Europe. Before we had gone a block Mrs. Morgan found the tag which proclaimed, "Made in Springfield, Massachusetts, U. S. A." We were chagrined that our European purchase had turned out to be an American importation, sold to us at a higher price than it would have been at home, but we were proud that here in Germany they knew the country to send to in order to get good pictures of fetching Dutch maidens. At Zurich I started to buy a little office fixture which I thought I had never seen before and which I intended to take home to surprise the Kansans, when I found out just in time that it was made by the Globe-Wernicke company of Cincinnati, and I knew we had the same thing for sale at The News office in Hutchinson. Hereafter in buying souvenirs of Europe we will look close for the brand.

This is the place where the "pâté de fois gras" originated. I do not know how many people in Kansas know what pâté de fois gras is and whether it is a flower or a dog. I had once seen the words on a bill of fare in a very swell restaurant, but the figures which followed the name were so much larger than those after ham and eggs that I stuck to "ham and." But when in Rome you must see the Forum, in Venice you must see St. Mark's, and in Strassburg you must have some pâté de fois gras. The food combination which the four French words stand for is based on goose-liver, and corresponds to about what we would call "goose-liver smothered in roses." It is very good, and you never forget the delicious taste or the price. Strassburg chefs make the stuff, can it and ship it all over the world to people who like delicate things to eat and who have sufficient credit to get a good stand-off. Pâté de fois gras is sweeter than chocolate, more luscious than peaches and more delicious than lemon pop at a Fourth of July picnic. It is a proof that Strassburgers have French stomachs as well as French hearts.

Speaking of eatables, we had the first loaf of bread in Switzerland that we had seen since we left home. After nearly two months on hard, stale rolls the sight of a reasonably good loaf of bread at Geneva made as strong an impression on my mind as Mont Blanc. Anybody who has traveled in Europe or in Arkansas will appreciate the feelings of a Kansan when he puts a slice of fairly soft bread between his teeth. It is better than pâté de fois gras, and it is almost exclusively an American institution.

IN OLD HEIDELBERG.

HEIDELBERG, GERMANY, July 22, 1905.

This is the old and famous university town of Germany. It is about two miles long and 200 yards wide, lying between the river Neckar and the steep hills which rise 500 feet high and which can only be ascended by terraced roads or a modern tunnel railway. The town is of comparatively recent origin, being really started only 850 years ago, when a Rhenish count who wanted to build a strong and impregnable fortress selected a spot 400 feet straight up the hill from the river and built the old castle of Heidelberg. Being thus the capital of a little German state, the Palatinate of the Rhine, it was an important place during the Middle Ages, and was fought over every few years for several centuries. In the fourteenth century the ruling count, whose title was Elector, developed a literary streak and founded the university, which became the center of learning and scientific study in Germany, and has continued so until the present day, although some of the newer universities like Berlin and Leipsig are now larger. The valley of the Neckar joins the valley of the Rhine here and makes a fertile territory and a prosperous city, but the university and the students are the main features of modern Heidelberg, now that counts, electors and castles are ruins or relics. There are many students in Heidelberg from America and other countries, but it is the rollicking German "yunkers" who make the life of the place.

German universities differ somewhat from American universities in the character and method of work. There are no recitations—only lectures and examinations. A student does not have to attend either. He can attend Heidelberg year in and year out and devote himself exclusively to the beer-garden and the dueling-ground. Or he can work hard, receive the ablest instruction and the highest degrees. The discipline of the common schools in Germany is severe—military in its character. But at the university the young man or young woman (for women now attend lectures at Heidelberg) can do as they please and go to Hades if they desire. The university buildings are plain and ordinary. The picturesque feature is the students, especially the young men who belong to the various "corps." Less than 10 per cent. of the students are members of these societies, but they color the town, for each corps has a distinctive cap,—red, yellow, white, etc. These organizations are the social life of the university, and at all hours of the day or night they are in evidence, parading with their caps and canes, occupying the beer-gardens and the promenade, jollying the girl waiters and having what is called in America a High Old Time.

Everybody has heard of the duel or sword-fighting. It is as much an institution at Heidelberg as football is at Princeton or K. U. Not many students take part in it, only members of the six corps, but it is the show feature of student life. Each corps has about twenty members. Each member has to fight at least one duel a term with a member of some other corps. This morning we went to the dueling-place just outside of the city and saw the game.

One gets a great deal of misinformation about this student dueling, but as near as I can find out it is done in a genteel and cold-blooded manner. When it is the turn of one of the corps members to fight he makes a face or refuses to salute a member of another corps. That constitutes cause for the duel, and the preliminaries are then arranged by the officers of the respective corps according to the rules and regulations that have come down through generations. The fighting is done in an inner court of a wine-garden. This morning there were ten duels on the program, and when we arrived the third was in progress. A young man of the bright-red-cap corps was trying to slice the face of a member of the dark-red-cap corps. Each was covered with felt armor, which protected all of his body, and also had goggles and nose-pad, a little bit more so than a football player. The seconds, very similarly attired, stood by the side of the principals and struck up the swords at the end of each round or when the blood came. The only unprotected places were the head and face, and the game was to slash the opponent there, not to stick him. Thrusting is evidently against the rules. A surgeon with an apron like a butcher attended to the cuts and the members of both corps stood quietly and calmly by, giving vent to no expression of feeling whatever. The officers of each corps saluted, the word was given, the two swords clashed away for a minute, and each fellow had a nice long cut on his cheek. When the round was over the seconds sponged the cuts. There is no specified number of rounds, but whenever the two seconds are satisfied that one man is cut enough the other is declared the victor and they salute and retire to get court-plastered or sewed up as is necessary. We saw four duels and got tired of the fun. In the last fought one of the men was apparently an experienced swordsman and his opponent apparently a beginner. (I understand that in order to show his courage a new man always challenges an expert.) After four rounds the face of the weaker swordsman was streaming with blood from a half-dozen cuts. I suppose he looked upon his defeat as a real victory because he showed the fellows that he could stand up and take punishment and never wince. Some people have curious ideas of greatness.

    They tell me no one is ever killed in these duels, but every member of every corps would be considered disfigured for life in America. Every one of them has long sears on his face and head. The restaurant where we eat is a favorite resort for the corps and we see much of them. It looks like a shame that every one of those bright young men will have to go through life with a face like a war map of Manchuria. But they wouldn't trade those sears for love nor money. (I am told they are good for love.) They are the badges of bravery and ability, and are as highly prized as the bronze button of the Grand Army man. As I have remarked, some ambitions are very funny, and if the German students want to be hand-carved in this manner there is no use of a football-, prize-fight-loving nation making any kick.

THE GERMAN WAY.

Heidelberg is a "wet" town. I suppose half the places on the main street are beer-gardens and some of the others are wine-rooms. Everybody in Germany drinks beer and wine. There is this difference between France and Germany: In France the men do most of the drinking as they sit in the sidewalk cafés watching the women go by. In Germany the man brings his wife and children and they all sit around the table in the garden or restaurants and drink beer. They do not seem to get intoxicated. I haven't seen anyone drunk, although they drink by the wholesale. Beer is high in Heidelberg, up to 2½ cents a quart, but out in the suburbs it is cheaper. I think beer-drinking makes the Germans have bad forms, for men and women get round and fat. But in Germany these forms are considered beautiful, so the sylph-like and the slender are looked down upon. It is an illustration of the fact that it is a good thing we don't all think alike about such things as personal beauty, or some of us would have to always be away back sitting down.

I have been in Germany a week, and I have not seen a half-dozen men smoking pipes. I thought Germans were great pipe-smokers, but they are not in this part. The Heidelberg pipes are mostly made to sell to Americans and English. The Germans smoke a little the worst cigars I have ever met. They are cheap in price and the Germans consume them in large quantities. The kind the high-class Germans use closely resembles a brand known in our country as "The Pride of the Sewer," and sells at about two for 5 cents. An American who is accustomed at home to buying "a good nickel cigar" can't find anything that good in Germany, unless it may be in the big hotels where they cater to American and English trade. I had always had Germans pictured to me as big fat men with long pipes in their mouths, sitting around tables on which were large steins of beer. The beer is here all right, but the men are as bright and energetic as Americans, and they smoke cigars and not pipes.

Another dream gone up in smoke.

It is a great country for castles and "legends." I think the average yield of legends per acre is larger in Germany than in any other country on earth, especially in the Black Forest and on the Rhine. That is one thing our country is short of—legends. Aside from a few old Indian stories, a tale of woe about the grasshoppers and reminiscences of the Populists, we haven't anything that approaches the legends which hang on almost every tree in the Black Forest and stick out of every castle-window. And yet Kansas could raise legends as well as Germany, for a legend is nothing but a lie told so often that nobody knows where it started; and Kansas has her share of liars. Here is a sample "legend" from the old castle of Heidelberg which we visited to-day:

A HEIDELBERG LEGEND.

The count of Heidelberg had a beautiful daughter. (They all do—in legends.) Her reputation for beauty went all over Germany and reached the shores of Great Britain. The king of England saw the photograph of the fair lady dressed in her bicycle suit, and instantly fell in love with her. But he did not want the German beauty to marry him for his money and title, so he disguised himself as a cook, got a job in Heidelberg castle and made eyes at the princess.

It was a case of two-hearts-that-beat-as-one, and the princess soon began to make dates and meet the supposed cook back of the castle and down on the Neckar. He revealed his real identity to her, but made her promise not to tell. He then went to the old man and asked him for the hand of his daughter. The count laughed at the cook, which made the latter mad and so he blurted out that the maiden loved him. Then the cook skipped out and the count sent for his daughter. She confessed to being in love with the cook, but on account of her promise did not tell his right name. The old count got into an awful rage and ordered his daughter whipped, and the lash was applied so well that the princess died. Before she passed away she told her father who the cook really was, and the count of Heidelberg was truly sorry; but that did no good. A few days later the king of England with an imposing suite arrived to ask the hand of the princess, and when he found out what had happened he took the old man out behind the barn and sliced him up in fine pieces.

There is a song which tells all about this affair, and the music is about as good as the legend.

WORMS AND OTHER THINGS.

Worms, Germany, July 23, 1905.

People do not laugh in Germany when you pronounce the name of this town properly. Say the word as if it were spelled Vorms and give the o the long sound, and you will admit that it is better than the way you used to say it. For many years I have heard of Luther and the Diet of Worms, and being at Heidelberg, only a few miles away, we came here to see Worms, the "Diet," and to spend Sunday. Four hundred years ago this was quite a town, one of the free cities of the Rhine owing allegiance only to the emperor. It was here that in 1524 Charles V., emperor of Germany, summoned Luther to appear before a congress of princes and imperial electors, and wanted him to fix up a compromise. The emperor of Germany was in a ticklish position. About half of his subjects were loyal to the pope and about half had bolted with Luther. The princes and dukes were divided, and were fighting each other to prove that they were right. The German empire was demoralized with internal dissension and feuds. So Charles thought it would be a smooth thing to get Luther before the august assemblage, induce him to concede some and get the Catholics to concede some, and have a sort of "Missouri compromise." Luther went to Worms, although he was warned not to do so. As a matter of fact, Luther did not want to separate from the Catholic Church, and his claim was that he wanted to reform it. But after the controversy had continued a few years he kept getting further away, and Charles had made his move too late. Luther laid down certain doctrines which he knew the loyal Catholics could not agree to, and then announced that he took his stand upon them and would not move. The result of the emperor's effort at peace-making was that each side was a little more infuriated than before, and the war went on.

A hundred years ago Worms had gone down to be a town of only 5,000 inhabitants, but now it has about 40,000 and is a thriving little city. But in spite of the growth and progress in the last century there is still a general air of quaintness and age which makes it very interesting because it is so different. A magnificent monument to Luther is the show feature of the place. On a massive platform ten feet high is the figure of the great reformer, over nine feet high, surrounded by statues of Huss, Savonarola, Wyckliffe and Waldus, and of princes who befriended Luther. A number of German cities are represented by allegorical figures or coats of arms, and the entire group makes an impressive monument and memorial. The palace where Luther met the emperor and princes has been destroyed, but another takes its place and with a right good imagination the tourist can stand where Luther stood, any day between the hours of 11 and 5 o'clock. Strange to say, the town to which Catholics and Protestants came is now controlled by the Jews, who dominate the business interests of Worms as they do those of many other German cities. Worms is on the Rhine river, and the valley of the Rhine is the garden-spot of Germany. Coming over the fertile fields of the Rhine valley is a good deal like riding in the Arkansas valley between Nickerson and Haven, with its rich farms, great orchards and prosperous communities. But in the hundred miles I have traveled along the Rhine I have not seen a reaper or a mower, a sulky rake or any other kind of machinery except a hand-sickle and a hand-rake. I think there are more women at work in the fields than there are men. Perhaps the men are off in the army. Perhaps they are in town drinking beer and talking politics.

Coming from Heidelberg to Worms we had to change trains twice in an hour's time. Changing trains is no easy job in a foreign country. At Manheim, where the station is as large and as busy as the Union Depot in Kansas City, our incoming train was late and when we arrived our outgoing train was due to leave. With the assistance of a porter I was handling a half-dozen grips and bundles when Mrs. Morgan discovered our train at the other side of the depot. She promptly started across the tracks just as she would at home. I thought there was a revolution or a fire, as a dozen train porters, as many policemen, the station-master and a lot of assistants set up a yell that fairly made the air tremble. The station-master rushed after her, caught up and brought her back, with at least ten men talking vociferously and gesticulating in German. The fact was she had broken the law of the empire. It is not merely violating a railroad rule to cross the track, but it is against the criminal law and punishable by a jail sentence. Of course they didn't do anything to Americans, but if a German should cross the tracks where it was forbidden they wouldn't do a thing to him! They actually held that train five minutes after time while we made a circuit of the station to the other side, when we could have sensibly and reasonably have been allowed to cross the track in a half-minute.

Speaking of railroads and the management makes me think of the conductors. I have ridden first-class, second-class and third-class in Germany. When the conductor enters the first-class carriage to see the tickets, he takes off his cap and says in German: "If you please, will you me your tickets show?" When he comes into the second-class carriage he says: "Tickets, if you please," and when you hand them over he gives them back with a military salute, but keeps his cap on. When he comes into the third-class carriage he simply says: "Tickets!"

When the train starts out of the station the station-master (dressed in a gorgeous uniform) stands on the platform at a salute until the last car passes him. This is a very pretty custom, and I think the station agents at Hutchinson ought to be required to put on their uniforms and salute the trains.

The almost universal custom in Germany is to eat out-of-doors in the summer-time. The hotels have spacious porches or gardens, and there we eat breakfast, dinner, and supper. (They have dinner at noon and supper in the evening in Germany.) There are no flies, and there seems to be but little wind, so you can eat comfortably in the open air and not swallow too much that is not on the bill of fare. It is a sensible and delightful custom. After the evening meal at the hotels or restaurants everybody stays at the table for an hour or so, and there is music by the orchestra or band. The only good feature I can see to the German army is that it provides nearly every city with a fine band which gives concerts frequently. The cities and towns usually support bands, and most of them own theatres and opera-houses. I think we have attended a band concert every evening since we entered Germany, and we could go in the afternoon if we had time.

By the way, right here in Worms, in the part of the city that looks about as it did in Luther's time, we were wandering down a narrow street when we were stopped by familiar music, the popular two-step, "Whistling Rufus." The German bands play a great deal of American music, mostly Sousa's marches or our "ragtime," and it always gets an encore. At Heidelberg the military band played "Hiawatha." For two years it has been almost against the law in the United States to play "Hiawatha." But the Germans liked it. I don't think the German bands play ragtime properly. They go at it seriously, as they do the selections from Wagner and such like which make up most of the program. They add a good deal of noise and they do not get the "swing" that is given by American musicians.

I have discovered in Germany that Wagner and his kind of composers wrote a lot of good music that never gets across the water, the kind that has tune to it,—not so much tune as Sousa's pieces, but a good deal more than is ever rendered in the United States. And I suppose the German bands understand Wagnerian music better than the American bands, just as Sousa can direct a better two-step or march than a German conductor. A German municipal band or military band, such as plays every night in one of the public parks in every city, is as good a band as Sousa or Innes ever took on the road. I am not a musical critic, I am thankful to say. I like music whether it is good, bad, or indifferent. I like grand opera some and light opera a great deal. I enjoy a fine band or a poor one, a selection from Chopin or a street piano. I will follow a band, a drum corps or a bagpipe all over town. I am even fond of the "Blue Bells of Scotland." Probably my recommendations will not be accepted by all the musical experts at home after these admissions, but I can't keep from saying that German band music is the best in this world to which I have been introduced.

I have written of the growing use of the English-American language on the continent of Europe. Here at Worms we are stopping at a very Dutch hotel. When the waiter came for the first time I went to work in German. The construction of a supper bill of fare in German is not easy for me, but I tackled the job bravely. I know enough German to order meat and potatoes, but my pronunciation is ragged on the edges and my verbs are not hitched right and the genders of the nouns are only likely to be right one guess in three. After I had floundered along for about three minutes the waiter gravely and politely interrupted: "Won't you please give me the order in English?"

RICH OLD FRANKFORT.

FRANKFORT, GERMANY, July 24, 1905.

This is one of the old and wealthy cities of Germany, with 300,000 people and a fine country around about. It is the place the Rothschilds came from. A few years ago when the Populists were pretty much the whole thing in Kansas and to be against them was to be in the pay of the Rothschilds and the Great Red Dragon, I was on the Rothschilds' side, and never having received any compensation I thought I would call and see what was the matter. It was no trouble to find the Rothschild house, for it is described in every guidebook and is marked by an inscription on the front. The morning after we reached the city we went to formally make a call, and found the place to be an old and unpretentious building. I rang the bell and asked the little girl who came to the door if Mr. Rothschild was at home. She ran away and I went on in and part way up the stairs, when a man appeared and said "fifty pfennig." I told him I was an old friend and merely wished to pay my respects —pay nothing else, not even fifty pfennig. I talked English and he talked German, but I had no difficulty in understanding that it would cost me 12½ cents American money to go through the house. This I declined to do, and unless the gentleman who wanted the fifty pfennig tells Mr. Rothschild I don't suppose he will ever know I came. In fact, I was afterward told that none of the present members of the Rothschild family live in Frankfort, but have their homes in Vienna, Paris, and London, where they dictate the financial policy of the world. Only a little over a hundred years ago the law of Frankfort was that every night at sundown and on Sundays and feast days all Jews must stay in their own part of town, and the gates inclosing their section were locked until the following day. As an illustration of how rapidly the wheel of fortune turns I was told that now, although comprising but one-tenth of the population, the Jews handle three-fourths of the business, own over half the real estate, and hold most of the high and responsible positions in Frankfort, where their great grandfathers had no more show than a rabbit.

Goethe, the great German poet, was born in Frankfort, and we visited the house of his birth and boyhood. His father was a lawyer, but the poet could not help that. Young Goethe was a bright lad, and took to writing poetry as readily as he did to going with the girls; and he kept at both occupations all his life. A petty German prince took him under his patronage and Goethe never had to work for a living, so he went on writing poetry and having a good time until he died at the age of 83 years. The Germans love Goethe as the Americans do Longfellow, for he was a poet who loved his country, his countrymen and his country-women, and his works are full of sweet and patriotic sentiment as well as being beautiful in construction. Goethe and his friend Schiller and the literary crowd which followed their lead, made the German language classical and correct, and occupy the same place in German literature that Shakespeare does in English. The "Goethe house" here is under the charge of a historical society, and has been put in the same shape that it was when Goethe was a boy. It is an interesting place, for it is not only full of mementoes of the poet but of the time in which he lived.

The most interesting public buildings I have seen in Germany are here, the "Roemer," a name applied to a group of twelve old and picturesque houses. In one of these the electors of the German empire (certain hereditary princes) would assemble to elect an emperor whenever there was a vacancy. After the election they would have a banquet and the fountain in the public square would run with red and white wine while the people cheered and drank the health of the new man. This was calculated to make the emperor very popular at least that night, but I wonder if the people were so enthusiastic when the headache came the next morning. These old buildings are well preserved. In fact, Frankfort is a city which takes good care of itself and is like a prosperous man. The most beautiful public garden I have seen is here, the Palm Garden, and a fine military band gives concerts afternoon and evening. Frankfort is not only well off, but old enough to enjoy the fact, and everywhere the city is made to look as handsome and be as comfortable as possible. The best and cheapest eating in Europe is in Frankfort, and that fact has made a deep and lasting impression on my heart.

It is doubtless repeating what has been said before, but I cannot help wonder at the industry of the German farmers. Of course they were raised right on the place, and their fathers and forefathers were farmers. They probably don't know anything else, and never expect to sell out and move to town. In this fertile Rhine country, where there seems to be a model climate, they irrigate the land as if it were arid and they fertilize and drain and cultivate with the hoe and rake. I never believed the story, but it is true. The wealth of a German farmer can be gauged by the size of the manure-pile in his front yard. No doubt when a German farmer brags on what he has done he does not refer to the purchase of a quarter-section of pasture land in the next township, but points with pride to the large and luxuriant heap of fertilizing substance which he can call his own. Instead of farming more land, he tries to get more out of what he has than he did, and his attempt is a success. He does not have a herd of cattle, but he has one or a half-dozen cows which live in the other end of the house, and are curried, fed and looked after as carefully as members of the family, perhaps more so. The cattle are good-looking, smooth and polished, evidently well bred, and certainly well taken care of. They are much better in appearance than the average of American cattle, but the care bestowed upon them easily accounts for the fact.

Frankfort is geographically in Hesse, the old state from which George III. hired soldiers to fight the Americans. In the good old times a little over a hundred years ago, a German prince who was hard up for cash would rent out his soldiers to fight and be shot at. The pay went to the prince, not to the soldier. It is hard to believe that such things occurred only a comparatively short time ago, and yet they did. The Hessians did not understand American tactics and were not much of a success in our Revolution, but they were always good fighters in German wars, and the little state was a powerful one. Frankfort was a "free city," and not under the active rule of the Hessian princes. For 500 years it kept its independence of any local prince, but in 1866 it was annexed to Prussia. The time for the independent cities of Europe was ended.

Besides Rothschild and Goethe, Frankfort is noted for the Frankfurter sausages. I was pleased to find that this was no legend. In Bologna, Italy, I was surprised to find no bologna, but Frankfort stood the test. There is also a house where it is said Luther preached a sermon while on his way to Worms. It is a tobacco-shop now.

In every German city there is an old bridge with a history. The old bridge at Frankfort across the Main river, which is a good big river and lined with freight boats, is mentioned in a document of 1222. It is constructed of red sandstone, and looks as if it would easily stand 700 years more. A bridge like that is really worth more than an art gallery. The legend connected with the bridge is not so bad. It seems that the architect who drew the plans and supervised the construction had made a mistake in his calculations. He came to realize that the span would not hold weight, and he could see the ruin of the bridge and his own reputation mighty close at hand. Of course he was in a terrible state of mind, and when he was at his worst the Devil dropped in to see him. The Devil offered to show him how the defect could be remedied, the bridge built and his reputation saved, if he would sign a contract that the first who crossed the bridge should become the Devil's property. The poor architect at first nobly refused, as most men do when tempted, and then fell, as men occasionally do. He signed the contract, the Devil pointed out the correction in the plan, and the great bridge was successfully finished. Then the architect had remorse (they always do afterward), and nearly went wild with thinking of what he had done. But the day the bridge was formally finished and turned over, before the mayor and city council could get into their carriages after the dedicating speeches, a rooster broke loose from a chicken-house, ran down the road, across the bridge and went to the Devil. Of course the Devil kicked, but the architect stood on the letter of the contract, and they all lived happy forever afterward. This legend is undoubtedly true, for on the middle of the bridge is an iron cross with a figure of Christ and on top of the cross is a bronze rooster.

DOWN THE RHINE.

COLOGNE, GERMANY, July 29, 1905.

The words "Down the Rhine" have a strong significance to everyone who has read history, poetry, or romance. From the time when Cæsar crossed the Rhine to punish the warlike tribes for invading Gaul, down to the Franco-German war of 1870, every European war has been fought more or less in the valley of the Rhine. And for 2,000 years whenever the nations of Europe were not marching their armies to the Rhine, the petty princes, potentates and powers of the valley were fighting one another. The Rhine is the dividing line in Europe. Those who have read these letters to The News will appreciate the fact that instead of going to the large cities of Munich, Berlin and Hanover, we began with the Rhine as it flowed out of Lake Constance and plunged over the falls at Neuhausen, and have followed it through the Black Forest and Germany on its way "down north" to the sea, and will finally watch it mingle its blue into the great salt water at Rotterdam and The Hague.

The last two days we have traveled by boat from Biebrich to Cologne, that part of the river which is called the scenic or "the castled Rhine," the part of which poets have sung and around which history and fiction have woven stories and legends in every language. But the Rhine is not only useful for the poet and the historian; it is also a plain business proposition. I am told and I believe that the Rhine carries more traffic than any other river in the world. It flows through a rich agricultural country, is lined with important cities, and especially with manufacturing places. Freight rates on the water are cheap. Products of the farm or vineyard, the shop or mill, placed on the boats, are carried with only one transfer to all the great markets of the world.

And now imagine the beautiful Rhine gliding among high hills, with every few miles a handsome castle or the picturesque ruins of one, with a busy railroad running on each bank, passenger and freight trains as frequent as suburban trains near Chicago, and two endless processions of steamboats, tugs and barges, one going up and one going down. That is the Rhine of to-day. The hills and castles reminiscent of the past, the black smoke of the furnaces and the shrill whistle of the engine the reminders of the present. You have to shut your eyes to see either the historic or the beautiful and keep them from "telescoping" into the practical present. And I will admit that the boats and the boatmen, the passengers and the freight interested me more than the dead-walls and the ivy-covered towers. If you think it over you will realize how castles and ruins pall upon your taste. When we began the trip we would rush from one side of the boat to the other to see a castle and hardly went below for lunch for fear we might miss a lofty summit or a breasted fortress. At the close of the trip a broken-down abbey or a roofless castle had no charms that would compare with a comfortable seat and a cigar. I remember well one of the last and largest castles we passed, one I had read of and looked forward to seeing. A friend enthusiastically exclaimed: "There is the Drachenfels on the other side!" And my coarse nature revolted, and I murmured that if the Drachenfels wanted me to see it, the Drachenfels would have to come around to my side of the boat. My neck was tired.

Really a homeopathic dose of Rhine castles would be very interesting. A thousand years ago some baron would build a big stone fortress high up on a hill overlooking the Rhine, and up to the discovery of gunpowder it was practically impregnable. The baron and his followers, according to the rules of the game, would divide their time between rescuing lovely maidens from giants and robbing the merchants and traders who passed by. I never heard of a knight or baron who worked for a living. History is filled with tales of deeds the old knights did for religion or for some fair lady, but it is silent or passes over lightly the fact that they made their money by robbery and murder, disguised under the name of expeditions, crusades, knight-errantry, and war. But when the inventive genius of man made a gun that would shoot through armor and discovered that gunpowder could knock down forts, the days of chivalry and highway robbery on the Rhine were over. The merchants and artisans no longer had to hire armies to protect their property and their families, and the rule of force was followed by the rule of shrewdness, a change which may not have brought perfection, but has resulted in a show of decency, fairness and honesty.

A few old castles transported from the Rhine to Cow creek or the Kaw would be helpful to the landscape of Kansas. But there would be no use of stringing them out for a hundred miles. A castle a thousand years old is interesting, always provided your imagination is good. The best way to enjoy castles is to believe everything the books and guides tell you. I am getting fascinated with the legends, although I think I can unfasten. Now here is a choice legend of the castles of the Two Brothers, which stand on neighboring hills and which I saw early:

THE TWO BROTHERS.

Once upon a time there were two brothers, both as valiant and noble knights as ever wore armor or robbed a traveler. Unfortunately they fell in love with the same girl, and as she couldn't accept both and had to say she would "always be a sister" to the other, the tension in the family circle got very tight. Finally the elder brother saw that the maiden loved the younger best, so he put his broken heart in his pocket, gave the pair his blessing and lit out for the crusades. In those days whenever a man lost out in love or was in danger of being hung for crime, he went to the crusades. The younger brother was very happy for a while, but he happened to visit another country and there he fell in love with another girl, just as much and as eternally in love with her as with the first one. The second girl was wise or else she had been warned of the young man's record, for she announced the engagement and the marriage followed soon. Girl No. 1 went to a convent with an aching heart, everybody settled down, and even the neighbors quit talking. Just at that time the elder brother returned from the crusades, and when he heard what had happened he thought it was awful. He went to his brother's castle and challenged him to fight a duel. The younger brother was worked up over the interference of the family in his private affairs and was anxious to fight. The two knights met in a plum-patch back of the convent and prepared to settle which was right. Just as they drew their swords the original girl, who had been informed of what was going on by some busybody, rushed out of the gate, threw herself between the brothers and begged them not to fight for her sake. She made such a good talk that they shook hands and took a drink together as a sign that it was all over. The elder brother offered to marry the girl in the convent, but she refused. The wife of the younger brother ran off with another chivalrous knight and the two brothers were left alone in the world. They built the two castles side by side, and spent all their days together hunting deer and wealthy travelers, and died without ever flirting with another woman (so the legend says). The ruins of the two castles side by side are evidence of the truth of the story.

THE LEGEND OF COW CREEK.

"Fair Bingen on the Rhine" was somewhat of a disappointment. Thousands and tens of thousands of American girls and boys have stood up in front of the school on Friday afternoons, scared stiff with the awful prospect of forgetting the next word, and told their school-mates:

soldier of the legion lay dying in Algiers,

here was lack of woman's nursing,

ere was dearth of woman's tears."

And when the same moon shone there that shone on fair Bingen on the Rhine, those countless American youths have breathed a sigh for the soldier and several sighs over getting through. Bingen is a good sort of manufacturing town, and the fact that the poet selected the name because of its rhythm and not because it fitted the situation accounts for the success of the poem. After some reflection on the subject among the storied regions of Europe I have come to the conclusion that it is the romancer and the singer who make a country great and interesting, and not any special merit of the place itself. If Cow creek had a few legend-writers in a few years it would rank with the Rhine, the Black Forest, and even the fields of old England. How would this do for a Cow creek legend, *a la* Europe?

LEGEND OF COW CREEK.

Once upon a time there lived on the creek a wealthy old farmer who had a beautiful daughter. The fame of her beauty spread all the way to Sterling and down to Pretty Prairie, and many young men aspired to the honor of her hand in marriage. Among those who loved her was a neighbor boy who had nothing to his credit but a good name and a rare ability to make speeches before the literary society which met every other Friday night at the schoolhouse. As the good name was no good on a check, he knew the old farmer would not listen to his suit but would likely kick him into the middle of next week if he asked him for his daughter. So all the poor young man could do was to see her home occasionally after church and talk about the soulfulness of love and the communion of congenial souls. The young lady really preferred the aforesaid young man, but as she did not want to undertake the job of making a living for two or more, and she knew her father would never consent to taking him to board, she could only sigh and pine and sit in the shade of a cottonwood tree and dream of love. At last the father told his beautiful daughter that he had selected a husband for her, a man from Nickerson, a man who owned two sections of land and a lot of oil stock, but who could not tell the difference between true love and a pain in his side. That night the two young people met down by the creek bank and she told him of the fate in store for her unless he got a move on himself. Their plan was formed. That night the lover braced himself with a good "bracer" and met the maiden behind the barn. Away they went toward the county seat with high hopes and enough cash to purchase a marriage license. Suddenly they heard the gentle murmur of the father, who had discovered the elopers and was telling the people for miles around what he would do to the son of a gun who was running off with his daughter. It was a race for love and for life, but the old man was getting the best of it and the lovers could hear him as he was overtaking them. They came to the creek, which was on its annual flood, and then they gave themselves up for lost. But the young man happened to look around and saw an old cow. An idea came into his head. He drove the cow into the creek and each of them grabbed her tail. She swam straight to the other side while the old man stood on the bank cursing a blue streak. Away they went to town and were married by the probate judge before the flood went down and the old man could get across.

There was nothing for the father to do but to give them his blessing and eighty acres of sand-hill land, on which they lived happily ever afterward. The stream which thus saved the lives and loves of those two young people has been called Cow creek ever since.

If the people of Kansas will take a few stories like the above, have them trimmed up and embellished, tell them to visitors and charge admission to see the relics, they will have as good a collection of legends as ever grew on the Rhine.

COLOGNE WATER AND OTHERS.

COLOGNE, GERMANY, July 29, 1905.

This is the place the eau de cologne habit started. There are over forty manufacturers who advertise themselves as "the original house" that first made this perfumed water. A few miles below here on the Rhine is the Apollinaris spring. I always supposed Apollinaris water came from the drug store, but there really is an original spring. It got its name from St. Apollinaris, who was a prominent church-worker a thousand years ago, and had his head chopped off by the heathen. The head is still preserved in a church and his name goes marching on with a label on the bottle. The highest cathedral I have seen in Europe is at Cologne, the top of the spire being 510 feet above the ground. It is a beautiful cathedral of Gothic architecture. The plans were made and a good part of the structure completed about eight hundred years before it was finished, the latter part of the job being done only a few years ago. The legend of the beginning of the cathedral is very authentic. The architect had spent several years on the drawings, but was not able to finish them satisfactorily to himself or the building committee. One night he had a dream, and in the vision saw just what had been lacking. But when he awoke he could not remember the design, and as is usual in such cases he said he would give anything to have it. The Devil promptly showed up and offered to reveal the wonderful plan if the architect would sign a contract to give in payment his own soul and also the soul of the first who should enter the church after it was completed. The architect tried to beat the Devil down on the price, but could not, and finally signed. The Devil lived up to his part of the contract, and the completed plans were so beautiful that the church authorities and the emperor and the city council were unanimous in declaring the architect the greatest man in his profession. As the church neared completion the architect began to worry. He took to drink, and went around carousing so that his friends thought he was crazy. Finally he confessed to the archbishop and it got into the newspapers, so the community was stirred up. No one was willing to be the first to go into the church, and yet if the great cathedral was to amount to anything, somebody must enter it. Finally a bad woman who was confined in jail sent word to the church board that she would be the victim. After due deliberation, and believing that she would go to the Devil anyhow, they accepted her offer. The day of dedication came. The people gathered from far and near. A carriage drove from the police station and backed up to the church door. Out of the wagon and into the building dashed a female form and the Devil in great glee grabbed, and broke its neck. But it was only a pig which the smart bad woman had fixed up in her clothes. So the Devil was cheated, the cathedral was dedicated, and all went right except for the architect, who was found with a broken neck and smelling of sulphur, for the Devil in his rage didn't do a thing to him.

Cologne has over 300,000 inhabitants and is a very busy city. This morning we went to the market. The grocery stores in Cologne and in all the German cities I have visited practically never keep green groceries. Everything of that kind is bought at the public market, which is a very interesting sight. From all the country around come the farmers and the farmers' wives with the produce of the garden, and from all over the city come the housewives or the maids, each with a big basket. The trading is brisk, and as it is nearly all done by women on both sides, there is some talk and the shopping habit is seen in all its glory. Then there is the fish market, the flower market, the poultry market, and even the old-clothes market. I am sure that in the big market-house and on the streets and the square in Cologne this morning there were two thousand vendors of goods, from potatoes to second-hand hats and from luscious fruit to old candle-sticks,—nearly everything conceivable that could be brought to the open-air market and sold. The market is still retained in a few old American towns, but to me it is a novelty with a never-fading charm, and in nearly every city where I have stopped the market has been a sight that I did not miss.

Next to the market the restaurant or beer-and wine-garden is the place to see the people. The Germans eat breakfast, dinner at noon, supper at 6 o'clock, and once more about 10 o'clock. From 7 o'clock to 10 o'clock the whole family sits in the public garden drinking beer or wine (not much, but long), listening to the music and getting hungry for the fourth meal of the day. There are restaurants everywhere—in the public buildings, the art galleries, the churches, on the sidewalks, and in the parks. I have not been to a German cemetery, but I would confidently expect to find there a garden with tables where one could get something to eat and drink.

The valley of the Rhine for more than a hundred miles is one vast vineyard, and the word valley includes the hillsides. The hills are high. The vines begin close to the water's edge, the vineyards being sometimes terraced and sometimes on a slope so steep that the men and women who cultivate them must wear climbers like telegraph linemen. It is a beautiful sight at this season of the year with the lofty heights clothed in green and pointing up into the blue sky, with brown old ruined taverns and castles and white châteaus and villas here and there among the green. One would wonder what could be done with all the grapes that must come from such a great vineyard if he did not look around him and see everybody drinking the juice and evidently endeavoring to keep pace with the production. At Coblentz the Moselle river joins the Rhine, and it is another charming valley full of history, poetry and grapes. Coblentz is old and quaint, with narrow streets, old-fashioned people, and the appearance of ancient days. On this trip I have seen a good deal of the German people. The class distinctions are about all that make them different from Americans. The poor folks always expect to be poor and do not move around with the aggressive action that ours do. I suppose I talked with a hundred, and every one of them wanted to come to America. Mechanics and artisans, very skillful, are not altogether satisfied with conditions, and they, too, talk America. But the great middle class of farmers and merchants are as full of patriotism and conceit as are true American citizens. They think Germany is the greatest nation on earth, and that all the countries will eventually admit the fact and take subordinate places. They don't like America or England, and they expect sometime to have war with us unless we give up easier than they anticipate. The typical German is not slow or easy-going, as he is often painted, but is energetic, pushing and "chesty." He thinks Germany can lick the United States with one hand tied behind, and is ready to have the work begin any time. In fact, Germans are just as offensively and ignorantly patriotic as are Americans, which is saying a good deal, for Americans in Europe nearly always go around with a chip on either shoulder, daring somebody to knock it off.

But the Germans are gentlemen. For the first time since I left Paris I saw men in the street cars give their seats to ladies. In Italy the rule is for the man to have first consideration. It makes American women furious when they meet Italian men on the narrow sidewalks to have to get off into the streets and let the gentlemen pass by. But they must do it or the men will simply walk over them.

In Germany the women in the country work in the fields and in the cities they are in the shops and offices more than in the United States, but they are treated decently and politely. The German is in fact more polite than the Frenchman. He even tips his hat to his man friends. If I go into a store to buy a cigar the proprietor or clerk who waits on me will say "good-morning" and "good-by." They do this with one another, and do not keep their company manners for strangers. German hotels are the best in Europe, and one of the customs is during the meal at hotel or restaurant for the proprietor to walk around and pleasantly greet his patrons, whether he knows them or not, on the comfortable theory that they are his guests. Germans are always willing to guide and advise strangers and they don't take "tips," at least not any more than in America. Germany is wealthy and prosperous as a nation and the Germans one meets when traveling are about the best folks you find in Europe.

In Germany a landlord advertises his hotel as "first-class" or "second-class." The second-class hotels are clean and good, but they have some mighty funny names. I had learned in England not to get worried over the signs of "The Red Lion," "The White Bull," etc. But German hotel-keepers go still further. They name their places after animals of all kinds and colors, and often saints and imaginary creatures. The Golden Calf, The Winged Lion, The House of the Weaned Calf, The Wild Man, were some of the names, but at Heidelberg one extreme was reached by the "Hotel Jesus," and at Worms the other extreme by the "Hotel of the Two Pairs of Drawers." I suppose every name has a story or a legend behind it and the name is a valuable asset of the property. Speaking of names reminds me that here in Cologne the street that leads to the market-place is called "Kingdom of Heaven street," and not far away is the "Grace of God street." I can see how these names might be properly used in Kansas, but they are out of place in Cologne.

HOLLAND AND BELGIUM.

IN DUTCH LAND.

AMSTERDAM, HOLLAND, July 31, 1905.

The kingdom of Holland is a little bit of a country, but it has exerted a great influence in history. In size it is 12,650 square miles, not as large as the Seventh congressional district of Kansas, but it has over 5,000,000 inhabitants and is busy from one end to the other. The greater part lies below the level of the sea, which borders it on the west and has been literally reclaimed from the water by the energy and work of the people. The Hollanders are the Dutch, and they have a saying: "God made the sea, but we made the land." The water is held back by immense dikes, and here in Amsterdam I look toward the sea and the great lot of shipping along the quay is higher than the tops of many of the houses; that is, the water is higher than the roofs in the town. The industry which has thus driven back and held back the sea has made little Holland a wealthy nation and Dutch capital has not only built up business at home, but it has gone into the farthermost parts of the earth, even to Missouri and Arkansas, constructed railroads, started factories and earned dividends or gone into the hands of receivers in large amounts. The country is covered with canals about as Kansas is with section-line roads. These canals are used for commerce, carrying freight cheaply, and for drainage, irrigation, and in place of fences. Every farm has its little canal leading to a main canal as a farmer's road in Kansas goes out to the main traveled road. The farmer brings his stuff to town in a canal-boat, and a farm-wagon is almost as rare a sight in Holland as a canal-boat is in Kansas. In wet seasons the canals are used as drains and in dry seasons as irrigating-ditches. Canals are built above the level of the land, so that irrigation is easy, and for drainage the water is collected in ditches and pumped up into the canals. All of these facts I had read about, as has everyone else, but to actually see such a country was like a dream come true.

There is more sky in Holland than anywhere else. The land is flatter than a Kansas prairie. The scenery would be absolutely nothing if it were not for the works of man upon the surface. There are no hills in Holland, no rushing streams, no picturesque bits of nature. Some of the land looks lower than the rest, but none looks higher, and the water from the big rivers that enter Holland on the east simply oozes through the soil and canals, without a perceptible current and really without river-beds or water-courses. The Rhine spreads out until it is fifty miles wide, but it is no longer a river,— merely a network of canals which it supplies with water, and its old channels are now made by dikes and drainage into farms and town-sites. The landscape thus becomes a flat, fertile country, mostly farmed in grass and pastured with cattle and sheep, a lace-work of canals in shiny streaks running in every direction, narrow red brick houses with white trimmings, and windmills which tower above everything else and stand like giant sentinels over the low and level country. These windmills are big, fifty to a hundred feet high, the lower part usually used as dwellings, constructed as strongly and stoutly as government buildings, and with four immense arms or sails which convert the Dutch zephyrs into horsepower. The windmills are used for grinding grain, sawing lumber and in all kinds of manufacturing, as well as to pump water from the low ground to the canals and into the sea. A Kansas windmill compared to a Dutch windmill would be like a straw beside an oak tree.

Very often in Europe I have been compelled to draw on my imagination to make the actual facts come within speaking distance of what had been written or promised about a country. Not so in Holland. Everything I have ever read about dikes, canals and windmills is true, and nothing you have been able to imagine is beyond the real existing condition and appearance.

Yes, there is one thing, and I wonder if other people would feel the same way. In the pictures and on the china the windmills, the cows and even the people have always been blue. Of course I knew better, but when I found that a Holland landscape was not blue and white, I felt as if I had been deceived. The sky is blue, but the windmills are browned with exposure, the cows are black-and-white, and the people are not any more blue in Holland than they are in Newton.

The ride from Cologne, Germany, to Amsterdam, down the valley of the Rhine, which is no longer picturesque or lined with castles and legends, gave me my introduction to Holland. Most of it is the kind of country in which a traveler can enjoy reading a good book. After the first enthusiastic demonstration over windmills,—and they are more numerous than telegraph posts along the Santa Fe,—and the excitement of watching canal-boats having died out, Holland is not a country that causes thrills. There is a strange effect created on seeing a canal-boat in a canal a little distance off. You see a sailboat or a steamboat apparently sailing right through a pasture. You can't see the water, and the effect is as if ships were really gliding over the grass and fields.

The canals are generally at least fifty feet wide and at least six feet deep. There are many good-sized boats. The power used is of different kinds: steam, sails, horses, men, women. Steamboats are numerous. Sails are used on nearly all, at least to help. Very often a man is hitched to a rope and sometimes a woman, with a regular harness so that the pull comes on the breast and shoulders. Dogs are not used to haul canal-boats, but they are the usual motive-power in the towns for small delivery-wagons, milk-wagons and the like.

CANALLING IN HOLLAND—THE EXTENSION OF WOMAN'S SPHERE.

The people of Holland, especially outside the cities, stick to their old peculiar costumes better than do the people of any other country in Europe that I have seen. The originals of the quaint Dutch pictures are here and numerous. The women wear the foolish bonnets, funny short full skirts, woolen stockings and wooden shoes, and the men the odd hats, clothes that bag between the hips and knees, and the wooden shoes that turn up like sled-runners. The wooden shoes are not worn in the house, but shaken off as the person enters and a pair of cloth shoes substituted. I suppose that is a ground rule made by the Dutch housewives, whose propensity for scrubbing and cleanliness is well known. But in spite of the deserved reputation, I do not think that Holland is as clean a country as it is advertised. The canals are close to being stagnant water, and as all the dirt and sewage goes into them there is an odor about Holland that comes near the smell you get from old cheese. Especially in the towns and cities where the canals form the principal streets, I can't escape the idea that they are a good deal like open sewers. The water is changed by pumping, but not often, and after it stands a while over the stuff thrown in one would think from the noticeable odor that it would breed sickness. They say it is not very bad, but it would cause a big kick in America—the newspapers would go after the city council a plenty for permitting such a nuisance.

A good deal has been said and written in the United States of recent years in regard to the "emancipation of women." The extension of civil and legal rights to persons of the female sex has been properly the subject of general congratulation. The club movement has done a great work in forcing a recognition of the work of women equally with the work of men. Prior to coming to Europe I had supposed that the women of the United States had made more progress along these lines than those of any other country. But I was mistaken. The women of Europe are far ahead of the women of America in the equality of the sexes. A women in continental Europe not only has the right to go out in the field and labor, but she can work on the roads, and she can engage in any business that a man can. In Italy I saw women harnessed alongside of dogs and in Holland I find them harnessed to canal-boats, the same as men. If there is any kind of work in Europe that a man can do in which women cannot and do not engage I have not discovered it, except the occupation of wearing military uniforms. The mercantile and shopkeeping business is almost entirely given over to women, and the right to carry trunks, shine shoes, sell papers and act as porters is not denied them. The men seem to be perfectly willing to let the women do the work, and the emancipation seems to have been accomplished without trouble of any kind.

The Dutch language is more like the English than like the German, with which it is classed. With my little knowledge of German I can read the Dutch signs and make a stagger at the newspapers, for there is more English than German in the written words. But the Dutch as a spoken language is like neither the German nor English. When two Dutchmen have a social, quiet chat it sounds like a buzz-saw. I can usually make a Dutchman understand me, but when it comes to my grasping the meaning of his talk I had as soon try to interpret the remarks of a file. It is ridiculous the way you have to change language every few hours' ride in Europe. But I quit trying when I came to the Dutch. They will have to talk English or make signs in order to get my money; and again I am brought to the conclusion that no matter what is the language of the country, "money talks."

THE DAM DUTCH TOWNS.

THE HAGUE, HOLLAND, Aug. 2, 1905.

Before leaving Amsterdam we took a trip through several little Dutch villages and to the island of Maarken, where the fisher-people continue to wear their eighteenth-century costumes in the progressive, stylish twentieth century. As a very pleasing incident of this journey we happened to reach Maarken at the same time with Queen Wilhelmina, so we not only got to see a live queen but in the excitement in the village escaped the attention usually given to American tourists by a thrifty people who have curios to sell. Queen Wilhelmina was a disappointment. I had been prepared to see a charming girlish sovereign, and I guess I was looking for something like a bright American girl with her hair hanging down her back. The queen is only 24 years old, but she looks 30. She wore a cheap-looking white suit which probably cost 30 cents a yard, American money. Her face was faded and so was her hat. She has large feet, wears coarse shoes, and her stockings wrinkled around the ankle like a fisherwoman's. The stolidity of the Dutch was too much for me. The queen walked through the village, and while everybody turned out to see her there was not a cheer. When she passed the little group of a half-dozen Americans we took off our hats and gave a loud hurrah, just to show our friendship. She didn't smile or look around, and we felt as cheap as she looked. In appearance she is sad and uninteresting. In America a governor or a president would have smiled and spoken cheerfully. But the queen of Holland does not have to run for reëlection, and I suppose that has a salutary effect on American statesmen. I will confess right now that my observations of European nobility have been made at a distance. I have not been mingling with the dukes and counts, but have received most of my impressions from the hotel clerks, the hackmen, the store-keepers and the workingmen. They are always glad to talk or make signs to Americans, and I have not met one laboring man who did not say he wanted to come to America. In the smoking-rooms and around the hotels I have talked some with the so-called "upper classes." They don't like America or England. I think the rulers of continental Europe and all the lords and valets are afraid America and England are going to combine with Japan and rule the world. The leading newspapers are full of that kind of talk, and while it is laughable to find that they think the American people are planning an invasion of Europe, it has a satisfactory side in the fact that it shows they think we could do it if we tried. The ruling classes are hostile politically to America. On the other hand, the working people are very friendly. The kings and nobles know that their jobs would not last long under American ideas. And the workingmen think that America means a chance to earn more than a mere living. Both classes have instinctively taken a position on the American question, and I don't blame them.

Amsterdam is the biggest city in Holland and is the capital, but the queen and court reside at The Hague. Amsterdam is rich in commerce, but is beneath the level of the sea, rather unsightly, and perhaps unhealthy. The Hague is about as high as the sea-level and is on real land, not the drained and reclaimed sort. It has some beautiful streets and thousands of acres of woods which are kept in comparatively original condition and used for parks and drives. The two cities are only an hour's ride apart, and The Hague is becoming the residence city for wealthy Dutchmen. Amsterdam is one of the financial centers of the world. The Hague is one of the political centers of the world. On account of its size Holland is not considered dangerous, and therefore presents a convenient meeting-place for international conferences. We visited the palace known as "The House in the Woods," where the peace conference was held in 1899, on the suggestion of the czar of Russia, and in which twenty-six governments were represented. The actual result was not much, but an international court at The Hague was provided to which nations can submit disputed questions if they wish, and probably after the Japs get through with the czar so he can call another peace conference, further steps will be taken to prevent or mitigate the horrors of war. Andrew Carnegie, the same gentleman who put up the money for the Hutchinson public library, has promised $1,500,000 to erect an international court-house at The Hague which will be a suitable place for what might be called an international supreme court. One great weight which every European power has holding down its progress is the necessity of maintaining a large standing army and thus withdrawing from active production a big per cent. of its workers. The governments of Europe know this and talk of "disarming," but each one is afraid the others won't do it. And I also have a guess coming that some of the kings and queens would worry a little over the future of their jobs if they did not have the big armies at their command.

The Dutch are a hard-working lot. They get up earlier than the people of any other country I have seen in Europe. And as the entire family works, from the grandmother to the dog, they accumulate wealth as a nation and as individuals. The ordinary dwelling is part of the store, the shop, the barn or the windmill, so that the women-folks can do their part of the labor and not lose much time going back and forth. Whenever the women are not attending to the farm or the shop they are scrubbing. The smell of good strong soap is one of the real Dutch landmarks as much as a windmill or a canal.

From Amsterdam we went to Edam and Monnikendam and Volendam and Zaandam, and from here we go to Rotterdam and through several other dams. The affix "dam" means bridge or embankment, and in a country of canals it is not surprising that nearly all the names of towns end with dam, Amsterdam being on the bank of the Amsel river, and so on. When I was a boy I heard the story of the teacher who was having her class give sentences containing the words they were learning to spell. One day they came to the word "cofferdam," and the teacher asked the bright boy of the class to frame a sentence illustrating the use of the word. He wrote on the blackboard: "Our old cow thought some sawdust was bran, and if she don't look out she will cofferdam head off." The word "dam" is not a cuss-word in Dutch. If it were, all the dam towns would be printed with a dash for the last syllable.

The history of Holland has about as much trouble in it as that of any country. It was not much of a nation during the dark and medieval ages, as there was no such state, but a number of petty vassal lords and bishops. About 1500 a Holland count got the title of Prince of Orange by marrying a French heiress. The principal ruler in Holland was the count of Burgundy, but the Dutch cities developed along business lines and were to a certain extent independent of kings and emperors, although nominally a part of the German empire. In the sixteenth century Philip of Spain inherited the sovereignty of the country, and by his bigoted and cruel rule started a civil war in 1568 which lasted eighty years and ended in the independence of Holland. During that war the Dutch had to have a leader, and so they elected William, prince of Orange, as stadtholder, or governor. Under his management the war was fought successfully, and when he was assassinated his son was elected stadtholder. The Dutch were divided into two parties, the Democratic and Aristocratic, and when Spain was defeated there was trouble between them. The so-called Dutch Republic was only an aristocracy, the privilege of participating in the government being restricted to a privileged class of small nobles and wealthy families. The office of stadtholder was elective, but generally went to the Oranges. Holland by its wise statesmanship and a strong navy was a world-power for a while, and in alliance with England and Sweden generally defeated the French and Spanish, and when there was war with England the Dutchmen held their own. Finally William III. of Orange became king of England, and the Dutch Republic lost its prestige. In the eighteenth century it was a tail to the English kite, and in 1806 Napoleon made his brother king of Holland and five years later annexed the country to France. After Napoleon's defeat the European powers created the kingdom of Holland, joined Belgium to it, and made William of Orange king of the united country. The Belgians broke away in 1830, and since that time Holland has been a monarchy, although the power is with the people.

I was much struck with the apparent lack of loyalty to the queen. In England everybody is loyal to King Edward because he not only represents the sovereignty of the nation, but he stands for the English constitution, rights of parliament and the people, and the king is the result of centuries of English thought and political action. But the Dutch have been without a king most of their history and they don't feel the reverence for the crown that the English do. Wilhelmina is not very popular, and her husband, who is a second-rate German prince that never mixes with the people and is said to be mean to his wife, is not liked at all. The Dutch cities have practical self-government, and it would not be surprising if after the death of Wilhelmina or in the event of some political upheaval the Dutch Republic would be revived on a broader basis than before.

ROTTERDAM, HOLLAND, Aug. 3, 1905.

To-day we came to Delft, where the Delft china does not come from any more, and from there to Rotterdam in a canal-boat. Riding in a canal-boat is a very pleasant way of traveling. If you want to get off, the boat simply runs up close to the bank and you make it with a jump—one jump is better than two. You glide along through the pastures and back yards and see the women scrubbing, the men smoking and the dogs pulling the carts. When you come to a low bridge everybody lies down flat until the boat is beyond it. Our canal-boat was propelled by steam, and we went flying along at the rate of five or six miles an hour, but still with plenty of time to inspect the country and visit with the people on the other boats if we could only have talked their language. As a cure for nervousness or as an antidote for being in a hurry I recommend a trip on a canal-boat.

Delft is a quaint old town, with old churches and clean canals. Two hundred years ago the manufacture of porcelain made the town famous, but for a hundred years the business was suspended and now most of the Delft china is made in New Jersey. Recently a factory has been started and real Delft ware can be obtained, but the American kind is just as good.

The canal-boat brought us through the town of Schiedam, where the celebrated Dutch "schnapps" is made. They tell me schnapps is closely related to that brand of American whisky which will make a man climb a tree. There are 200 distilleries in Schiedam. The Dutch are given to strong drinks rather than beer. The result is that the Dutch get wildly and meanly drunk, whereas the Germans merely get fat.

Near Rotterdam we canalled by Delfthaven. This is the place from which the Pilgrims sailed for North America in 1620. They stopped en route in England, but their original start was from here. They had come to Holland from England in order to secure freedom of worship, but they were still Englishmen and did not want to become Dutch. So they secured a promise that they would not be disturbed in the New World, and left their Holland home. If they had stayed in Delfthaven there would have been no New England, no Bunker Hill, no United States. But they did not stay.

THE KINGDOM OF BELGIUM.

BRUSSELS, BELGIUM, Aug. 5, 1905.

I do not suppose other people are as ignorant as I was, but I will admit that in my mind I have always lumped off Holland and Belgium together as two countries with the same kind of people, the same language, the same habits and generally the same government. This is a great mistake. Holland and Belgium are about as unlike as the United States and Mexico. Holland is Dutch, with a language related to the German and English, and with Teutonic characteristics. Belgium is allied to France, the people speaking French or a kind of French, and with traits of character like the Parisians. Holland and Belgium have never agreed well politically and have never lived together harmoniously. When the allies had defeated Napoleon they created the kingdom of Holland and Belgium and tried to tie the two together. The combination lasted just fifteen years, and in 1830 the Belgians revolted, declared their independence and fought successfully to make it good. This year they are celebrating the seventy-fifth anniversary of Belgian independence. Two hundred years ago the king of Spain was sovereign over both countries. Holland threw off the yoke and did business on its own account, while Belgium failed and remained the property of Spain or Austria down to the time of Napoleon. The Hollanders drink "schnapps" and the Belgians drink wine. The Hollanders are Protestant in religion and the Belgians are Catholics. Except for the fact that they are side by side along the North sea and are flat and low, the two countries differ in about everything possible.

The largest city in Belgium is Antwerp, located on the Scheldt river a little way from the sea, and with one of the largest and best harbors of Europe. During the Middle Ages Antwerp was a great commercial city, monopolizing much of the trade with the Orient, and being known everywhere for its wealth and business. In the eighteenth century, under Spanish and Austrian rule, the city lost its standing and went down to about 40,000 population. During the nineteenth century it had a boom; now there are 355,000 inhabitants and Antwerp looks like a great American city,—with many wide avenues, beautiful buildings, and handsome stores. Aside from the fact that the streets are often narrow, a modern city in Europe looks better than one of the same size and standing in America. The Europeans have better ideas of architecture, put up their buildings more substantially and with more regard to their appearance, and have less of the cheap and shoddy construction than we do. I suppose we have as good architects in America as in Belgium, but I know of no city in our country where the business blocks are so elegant or so well built. Our folks build in a hurry. Over here they build for centuries, because they have already had centuries and know that is the way to do. I haven't seen a frame house except in Switzerland. When people build with stone they are apt to put the work there to stay. And these modern European cities, by which I mean cities which have kept pace with the world's growth and are not simply living on history and tourists, have many large squares with monuments and fountains, parks with gardens and boulevards with drives,—all over the city, not simply where the rich folks live as in some American cities. I reckon I am as conceited about my country as anybody, but I get it taken out of me every now and then, and modern city-building is one of the places. It would pay our town-builders to take a little more time and do better, more substantial and more tasteful work.

Brussels is the capital of Belgium. If all the suburbs were taken in as in Chicago and New York, it would have a half-million people. It has the reputation of being one of the handsomest cities of Europe, and is called "the second Paris." It has many wide avenues, beautiful shops, and the people, like those of Paris, are great on having a good time. Nearly every other store in Brussels is a lace store, and most of the rest are jewelry stores. There are said to be 150,000 women in Brussels and vicinity making lace for sale, and they are paid by the shops for which they work about 20 cents a day. The country round about is fertile, but the farming is more what we would call market gardening. The picturesque costumes have disappeared, and the Belgians dress and act more like French and Americans than any other European people I have seen. Their farm labor is still crude. There is no machinery, and there need be none so long as labor is cheap. The dogs pull the carts to town with the truck for market and the working-people live on fish and vegetables because they are used to it and because meat is away beyond their means.

To-day I went to the battlefield of Waterloo. It has always been a matter of regret to me that Napoleon did not win that fight. The big powers of Europe had combined and forced his abdication. They sent Napoleon to Elba and were quarreling over a division of the spoils when he escaped and returned to France. The people received him with joy and his old soldiers rallied to his standards. The allies ran hither and thither and were scared almost to death—all but the English, who never know when to quit. Wellington with about 70,000 soldiers was near Brussels and Napoleon rushed his army of the same size to meet him. If Napoleon had defeated Wellington the backbone of the alliance against him would have been broken and the map of Europe would have been very different from what it is. The battlefield is comparatively small. The two armies had a front of about two miles and were less than a mile apart. In those days a cannon could not shoot a mile and a musket not more than 150 yards. After the first firing the guns had to be reloaded, so as a matter of fact there would be a few volleys and then the opposing armies would clinch and go at it with bayonets, clubbed muskets, and swords. That was the way at Waterloo. Napoleon made the attack and Wellington's army had the help of stone walls and position. In a space of about forty acres around one farmhouse there were 6,000 killed and wounded. Both sides fought like the devil, or rather like devils, and took few prisoners. The English allies held their ground all day, beating back the frequent and ferocious French charges. In the evening the Prussian army under Blucher came slowly up at one side and the outnumbered Frenchmen had to retreat. It was all over with Napoleon, for his army was dead or missing; so he again gave up, and this time his enemies were careful to put him at St. Helena where he could not get away.

A great monument was erected on the battlefield by the victorious nations. It is a mound of earth 150 feet high, pyramid-shaped, and a half-mile around the base. On top of the mound is a figure of a colossal lion. The mound is the highest point for many miles, and from its top the entire battlefield is easily seen. It is a very impressive sight. When the great mound was constructed the earth was carried in baskets by women who were paid 8 cents a day. That kind of a price for labor makes a steam shovel sick. The people who live around the battlefield have a rich tourist crop. Although they are Belgians I think some of them are descendants of Napoleon's soldiers, judging from the way they charge. Just about the time the visitor gets excited or interested in the historic spots, he is reminded that there is "something for the guide," or that he can buy maps, picture cards, bullets, buttons from Napoleon's coat, or get a drink of water from the well in which the bodies of 150 French soldiers were thrown.

Belgium is one of the busiest countries in Europe, but labor is really not better paid than elsewhere. A laboring man gets 30 cents a day, skilled laborers up to a dollar. A woman works at lace-making for 20 cents a day, or a woman will come at 7 o'clock in the morning and work until 8 o'clock in the evening, a Belgian working-day, for 20 cents. The cost of good, decent living is not much if any less than in Kansas, but of course people who earn only 20 or 30 cents a day don't live well. Their home is with the cow or the dog or with people just as poor, and a beefsteak would probably give them the gout. I have seen similar conditions in the slums of American cities, and once, when the tariff bars were thrown down and our factories put to competition with Belgian and other European factories where labor is paid as I have stated, there was a temporary paralysis of labor attended by suffering and want. But these are the normal conditions in Belgium and in Europe at a time which is considered one of general prosperity. I wonder how it must be with hard times. The "bugaboo" of "competition with pauper labor" is not a political imagination, but would be a sad reality if the American people should vote for a change in the tariff policy. I have learned this lesson from the mouths and faces of the workingmen of Europe.

Of course there are American-made goods that come into Europe. They are all here because the Europeans have nothing near as good. The American typewriter, the sewing-machine, the Wernicke office supplies and the American shoe are always advertised boldly and freely. Other American wares are sold without the American label because of some prejudice, especially in England. In order to show my patriotism I started lifting my hat every time I saw the sign or advertisement of American goods. At first I enjoyed the novelty, but as I learned to look for the marks I soon had my hat off most of the time. I didn't mind honoring any American article, but it grew wearisome to have my hand bobbing up to my hat whenever I turned around, especially as Carter's liver pills and Quaker oats have just covered Europe with their posters and their catch-lines. When the American does start to do business in Europe he does it right, and is not afraid to put his name on any place the police will let him. And it is comforting to a pilgrim in a strange land to see in big letters on street cars and fences the names that decorated the old walls and billboards at home.

EUROPEAN ART AND GRUB.

BRUGES, BELGIUM, Aug. 8, 1905.

In this quaint old town we are spending the last day of our stay on the continent of Europe. To-morrow we sail from Ostend to Dover, and the prospect of a return to a land where the English language is spoken is next to getting home.

Of all the cities of the Netherlands, Bruges has best held on to the ancient appearance and ways. The fact may be explained by the figures. During the boom in Belgium a few centuries ago, Bruges had a population of 200,000, while now there are only 54,000. There was no necessity to tear down the old buildings to make room for modern structures or provide wide boulevards and promenades. Consequently the old buildings stand, only modified in appearance by the wear and tear of weather and years. The sole business of the town as near as I could see is lace-making, and as the women do that there is little left for the men, except to drive cabs and hold the offices. We walked down a little narrow street, perhaps twelve feet wide, lined from one end to the other on this pleasant day with women sitting on stools making lace. The advent of a few Americans almost caused a riot in the desire to see and be seen, and the little street seemed to swarm with women and with children. Working over the pillow these women make lace to be sold at 15 or 20 cents for their day's labor. Girls hardly into their teens and grandmothers up in the 80's were laboring side by side. One old lady with whom we had a most delightful visit, although neither could understand the other's language, and from whom Mrs. Morgan bought some of the handiwork, is 86 years old, and yet she cheerfully and ably manipulates the hand-shuttles that make the lace as if she were not half that age. There is a special provision of Providence that nearly always applies. These women of all ages who have to make lace or starve, work in abominable light and yet have excellent eyesight and never wear spectacles or glasses. In America, where the lace is bought and where such work is a delicate, eye-trying task, the women have trouble with their eyesight and must have artificial help to see the lace that the Belgian women make. The wind is tempered to the shorn lamb.

Bruges is also the depository of the earliest specimens of Dutch and Flemish art, for here nearly 500 years ago lived Jan Van Eyck, and he and his brother were the pioneers in the style of painting which is generally known as "Dutch." They were followed a few years later by Rembrandt, Rubens, Van Dyck, De Crayer, Jordaens, and their crowd, who went to Italy and learned a good deal, but who were really followers of the Van Eycks. I have spent some time in the art galleries at Amsterdam, The Hague, Antwerp and Brussels, and have picked up a smattering of knowledge of Dutch and Flemish art which I would like to unload. The "whole shooting-match," as the Germans would say, is generally called Dutch, but there is a perceptible difference between the work in Holland and Belgium, although the artists lived so close together that they naturally formed one great school. Peter Paul Rubens, who generally gets first place, was a Belgian, although he was born out of that country when his parents were politically exiled. He lived at Antwerp and was brought up in a Jesuit school in a Catholic country. Rembrandt was a Dutchman, born at Leyden, Holland, and a politician as well as an artist in a Protestant country. If one will reflect upon the religious situation in Europe in the early seventeenth century, he will see that no matter if both used the same colors and the same rules for drawing, they were bound to treat different subjects, or have different conceptions of the same subject. Van Dyck, the third of the celebrated trio, was born in Antwerp, but went to London, and there did most of his work in portrait-painting, his specialty, because he was better paid by Englishmen. The Catholic Rubens and his followers painted for the churches and cathedrals, and for a Catholic constituency, and usually portrayed religious subjects, while Rembrandt and his pupils painted for the Dutch burghers, and their best pictures are of men, grouped in military companies or trade guilds. Rubens is more ideal and spiritual, Rembrandt more material and human. Therefore it is that people who like one often do not appreciate the other. I really like the Dutch art better than the Italian, although it is a good deal like a boy trying to decide whether he will have cherry pie or custard pie, and wanting both. The influence of environment and education is clearly seen in the fat Madonnas and the pictures of public-houses and drinking-bouts which are favorite subjects. The Dutch artists also lean to "realism," and about nine times in ten a picture of the realist school is unpleasant and therefore to my mind inartistic. For example, one of Rubens's great masterpieces represents the martyrdom of a saint who had his tongue torn out, and in the picture the executioner is handing the red, bleeding tongue to a dog. Another picture shows an execution, the axeman holding up the head, and the body with the stump of a neck the main feature of the foreground. Some people like this sort of thing, but I don't. For a hundred years after Rubens and Rembrandt, the Netherlands produced no art, at the time the countries themselves were demoralized and the prey of the larger powers. Recently Dutch art has revived in the portraying of Dutch landscapes, windmills, canals and such, and to my mind it is the pleasantest and most effective art now alive in Europe, away ahead of the Italians, who persist in imitating the old masters and tackling subjects which have been thoroughly covered so much that there is hardly a chance for a new impression.

Every town of any size in Belgium and Holland has a public art gallery, and the people ought to be artists merely from association. But as a matter of fact three-fourths of the visitors to the galleries when I was there were Americans and English.

Speaking of art reminds me of hotels. Before leaving Europe I want to pay a tribute to the hotel-keepers of the continent. I must have been wrongly impressed by what I had read and heard, for I had looked forward with dread to the queer ways and the strange dishes I was to go against on the trip. As a matter of fact the hotels in Europe are better and cheaper than those of America. The management is more courteous, the service better, and the eating far surpasses the equivalent in the United States. The "tipping system" is not bad at all and the effort of the landlord to get at your money is concealed by a show of cordiality and hospitality which I have never experienced in a strange hostelry in my own country. I am overcharged and worked ten times more in Kansas City, Chicago and New York than in Rome, Cologne, Brussels, or any other European city.

When a traveler arrives at a continental hotel he is greeted at the entrance by the hall porter or clerk, and instead of being bulldozed over a counter by a gentleman with a diamond stud into paying twice the ordinary price for a room, he is quietly and pleasantly told what rooms are vacant, what are their rates, and allowed to make a selection. He does not have to tip a porter or a bell-boy for every little favor. From the proprietor to the "boots" everyone in the hotel is at your service and nothing to pay—not then. Of course you expect to do the right thing when you leave, but for the time this cordial service seems to be spontaneous and animated with a sincere desire for your comfort. In Germany the proprietor of the hotel keeps up the pretense that you are his guest, and every day he inquires after your welfare. In the German restaurants the proprietor walks around and speaks pleasantly to everyone and you feel that he is really glad to see you without associating that sensation with the payment of the bill. Everything and everybody in the hotel is at your service. There is always a reading-room with newspapers, often American papers, smoking-rooms, lounging-rooms, and comfortable parlors where it is a pleasure to spend the time. In nearly every hotel there is a free library, mostly books of the country, but always some in English. At the Parker House in Boston, my last stopping-place in America, I had been surprised and delighted to find a well-selected library for the use of the guests of the hotel. I supposed that was a Boston innovation and was prepared to brag about it, but I have found a similar library in nearly every hotel at which I have stayed in Europe. An American hotel does not give half the space to the general use and comfort of guests that a European hotel does, and what it does offer is usually only a big office and stiff parlors in which people stay only when they can find nowhere else to go.

European cooking is far ahead of American cooking. A cook in this country is not an accident, not a man or woman who is cooking until a better job offers. A cook is something between a professional man and a skilled mechanic, and young men learn the business as thoroughly as they do engineering or banking. Labor is cheap, so that in the kitchen as well as in the front rooms there is always plenty of service, and it is by people who are brought up to it and not by boys or men who are down on their luck. I expected to be "fussy" over the cooking and cookery, but I have hardly had a poor meal in Europe and not a bad one at all. There is not much difference in the stuff used or in the way of serving, but the work is better done, and all the good American dishes like beefsteak and eggs are found in Europe looking as natural as life. The Europeans do more with mutton, veal and fish and less with beef than our cooks, and the small farms raise vegetables that are delicious.

When one leaves the hotel the proprietor or manager always comes to see him off and say good-by. There isn't such a crowd of servants waiting for tips as is generally alleged. Your porter, who has polished your shoes and carried your baggage, is on hand, and the chambermaid casually meets you on the stairs. The head waiter expects a tip and so does the hall porter, and there are usually a couple of other attendants ready to receive, but not obnoxiously so. I learned that the best way to do was to be as polite as the Europeans. A few minutes before time to leave I would say good-by to the head waiter, the smoking-room attendant, and any other who had rendered special service, giving each a small tip which he always took with many expressions of good-will and appreciation. That prevented any assemblage at the door when we left, and the last good-bys and tips were only expected by the man who brought the baggage and the hall porter who put us in the carriage and gave me full information as regards the coming journey and the next stop.

The rates at European hotels are much less than in ours. The prices for rooms are about half what they would be in America for similar accommodations in the same-sized places. The restaurant prices are a little less than ours. I should say that in Europe you pay about $2 to $3 a day for what would cost $3 to $4 in America. In small hotels and boarding-houses the same ratio is maintained, and there is no doubt in my mind that "room and board" on a European trip for an American is little more than half what it would be for a European in America. In these prices I include tips. The ordinary American will greatly enjoy life on the continent, provided, of course, he does not always eat at the "table d'hôte," or regular meal-table, which is monotonous everywhere. And also he must not want a room with a bath, or an elevator. Very few buildings in Europe have elevators, and the natives do not use them. It is an inconvenience to walk up two or three flights of stairs to your room, but in the hotels that do not have "lifts" you must remember that is the way the nobility and everybody does in Europe, and quit kicking. You can get a bath in the bathroom or you can scrub yourself with the contents of the washbowl, after you have had some experience. That is the custom of the country, and the thing to do is not to be telling about the rooms with baths in America, but accept the situation, look pleasant, and you will get along all right. It is the same way in Europe that it is everywhere else in this vale of tears: if you look for trouble you easily find it, and if you are constantly talking and thinking of the conveniences which American customs have provided and which are not used in Europe, you can make yourself miserable and unpopular. But if you accept the ways of the country, enjoy the novelties even if they seem old-fashioned and strange, you will have a grand old time and will make yourself solid with the people.

In Europe the name "United States" is rarely used. We are "Americans." The people of Canada are Canadians and the people of the United States have the sole use of the title of Americans. They consider us the whole thing, and we always admit it without argument. There is a general impression in the Old World that all Americans are rich. There is a general impression that sometime we will fight the rest of the world, and I think there is an impression that we will lick. So far as I can see, Americans are treated about as well as dukes, and the ways of traveling are greased for them by everybody along the line. (Grease to be paid for, of course.) In two months' travel on the continent, usually not knowing the language, we have never missed a train or connection, been mistreated or imposed upon, allowed to suffer inconvenience or annoyance. That is a record it would be hard to equal in America.

ENGLAND.

IN OLD, OLD ENGLAND.

WARWICK, ENGLAND, June 12, 1905.

When the American tourist reaches old England he has a large and well-selected stock of emotions which he can feel, in addition to the thanks in his heart that the short but "nahsty" trip across the Irish sea is at an end. No matter where an individual's ancestors may have come from, the mother country of America is England. Up to 1776 our history was only English history, our customs English customs, our laws English laws, and when the Continental army began shooting at the British soldiers, the Continental Congress accompanied every volley with a resolution declaring that the colonists had no desire to separate from England, but were only fighting in self-defense. Our laws, our language, our literature are English. The fight of the parliament against the crown has reached practically the same result in England that the revolution of Congress against King George did by a short cut.

This is the land of Shakespeare, Milton and Dickens, who are just as much American as English, except for the accident of birthplace. This is the home of our heroes of medieval times, of Ivanhoe, Richard the Lion-hearted, and the Black Prince. This is the country which is familiar to us by name and history through Scott and Thackeray, Dickens and Lytton, and a hundred other authors whose works are read in the American homes. We are not strangers to such names as Kenilworth, York, Shrewsbury, Chester, Stratford, Oxford, Cambridge, and in fact nearly every town on the map of England. This is more like the visit to a long-absent friend and not an entrance into a foreign land. We are now going among places of which we have read and among the monuments and works of men whom we have held close to our hearts through the pictures painted for us by our authors. We are going to actually see the things we have so often read about and which we have so much dreamed about.

Instead of beginning at London, the great center of trade, we are going to begin here at Warwick, the center of the oldest Old England left on earth. In Warwick we are five miles from Kenilworth, the castle Scott made famous, seven miles from Stratford-on-Avon, where Shakespeare was born, and surrounded by beautiful rural England, with a fine old castle only five minutes walk away, and churches and buildings which were old when Columbus discovered America.

The first stop in England was at Chester, which was a town of importance when Julius Cæsar was doing business. The walls the Romans built were demolished by the Saxons but rebuilt, and Chester was the last place in England to surrender to William the Conqueror. During the Middle Ages it was the scene of more fights and sieges and the walls then completed are the same walls which we walked on this week. The walls are from ten to twenty feet wide at the top, twenty to thirty feet high, and little towers occupy the angles and corners. From the wall of Chester Charles the First saw the parliamentary army defeat his soldiers, and when Chester surrendered, Cromwell's men had all of England.

There are two main streets in Chester, crossing each other at the center of the town and terminating in the four city gates. All the other streets of the old town are alleys from six to ten feet wide. But the curious part of Chester is "the Rows." Along a good part of the main streets there is a second floor, or rather a stone roof over the sidewalks. On this upstairs street are stores and shops, and business is going on as briskly along the second story as on the ground floor. As there were originally but the two streets in Chester, the people simply doubled the street capacity,—a thousand years ago and they haven't changed. In fact, I suppose a great many people in Chester who have never been out of the neighborhood, think that is the proper and usual way of arranging business streets in all towns.

The greatest place in England is Stratford-on-Avon, because Shakespeare was born there. A great many English towns have ancient cathedrals and are the birthplaces or the deathplaces of kings and queens, dukes and ministers, but Stratford is the only place where Shakespeare was born and there has been but one

Shakespeare. Many great men have several birthplaces, or perhaps I should say, several towns claim to be the only birthplace. But Stratford-on-Avon is a thousand years old or more, and has never done anything for the world except to provide William Shakespeare, and the world says that is enough to last another thousand. I stood in the church and saw the slab which covers the dust of the great poet and man-knower. By his side are the graves of his wife and daughter. Around the chancel are the inscriptions and memorials which tell of the admiration and affection of the world.

The house where the poet was born is now owned by a public association, and great pains have been taken to gather all the relics of his lifetime that have been spared. The rooms are arranged just as they were when his father, a highly respected tradesman who reached the dignity of a justice of the peace, was running his little shop and William was poaching in the neighboring fields and streams and sparking Anne Hathaway, whose home was a mile away. The Hathaway cottage is kept in the same way as the Shakespeare house, and we wandered through the low rooms and up the narrow stairs just as they were nearly four centuries ago. In talking with an Englishman at Warwick he said he believed the Americans thought more of Shakespeare than the English did, for more of them went to Stratford. Of course that is hardly correct, for the English all love Shakespeare, but they probably do not visit his birthplace so much as American travelers do. Practically every American goes to Stratford, some of them perhaps just because the others do. Coming over on the ship I was being enlightened by an aggressive American on just what was what. "Going to Stratford?" he said. I assented. "Yes, you'll go there and look around and wonder what in hell you went there for." But that is not the sentiment which fills the hearts of most of the cousins from across the ocean, as is evidenced by the reverential awe and the thorough appreciation of every nook and corner shown by them when they are in the historic village.

The river Avon is about the size of Cow creek, and looks a good deal like it. The banks are low and the meadows and fields come right to them, without the timber that borders most American streams. The town of Stratford is old-fashioned and quaint. Just as in Warwick, the hotels or inns bear such names as "The Red Dog," "The Bull and Cow," "The Golden Lion," a style of nomenclature which I had always half-way thought was imaginary with the great authors who have made such names familiar. Large, stately trees line the roads and stone walls and hedges conceal the fields and farms, revealing just enough to enhance the beauty of the landscape. One can dreamily think as he rides in the coach from Stratford to Warwick that he is back in the days of Queen Elizabeth and half expect ye knights and ladies to appear before the gate of Kenilworth, but as he does so there is a sudden whir-r-r, a cloud of dust and a smell, and the automobile of the twentieth century has rudely broken the dream.

We visited the castle of the earl of Warwick. The earl evidently did not know we were coming, for he was away, but a shilling admitted us through the big gate in the massive stone walls which surround the castle and inclose probably twenty acres of ground. It was originally built by a daughter of Alfred, about 915, and has been more or less knocked down and built up since. It is said to be one of the finest old castles in England. A regiment of soldiers could easily parade in the large court within the walls and be quartered in the building and towers. Many a time such a garrison has occupied the place, for the earls of Warwick have been fighters from the beginning and Shakespeare's Warwick was a regular Cy Leland or a Stubbs in his day, and was known as the king-maker. The castle is about twice as large as the Hutchinson Reformatory, and the earl has to keep a good deal of hired help in these times of peace. Many of the great rooms are kept just as in the old days of chivalry and are filled with armor and weapons. The banquet-room is maintained as it was in the great earl's time, and much of the castle is really a museum and gallery full of the pictures, portraits, furniture and tapestries of the long ago.

Kings and queens, earls and earlesses, have walked the halls and had their brief time upon the stage of life. The noble of to-day does not have the armor or the power he did then. His band of armed retainers has changed to a crowd of peaceful laborers. He does not lead his men to war, but presides at country fairs and acts as dignified as the spirit of the twentieth century will permit. He no longer fears a midnight assault from a neighboring baron, but only dreads the ravages of the American tourists and sensibly compromises by letting them ravage at a quarter apiece. The times of chivalry are gone.

eir swords are rust;

ǝ knights are dust;

ǝir souls are with the saints, we trust."

Here in Warwick and at Kenilworth we take a long dream backward, and by working our imagination and our sentiment we see the England of Shakespeare, of Warwick, of Ivanhoe. It is a good dream, but it is a past that will never return, a past that is more nearly connected with the present in Warwick than at any other place. It is old England, which first learned to rule herself and then began to rule most of the rest of the world, and with the assistance of the American child will undoubtedly do the business in the future. We are going to London and Liverpool, the castles of commerce and industry which now command the trade of the globe. In the England of to-day the castles of the business man and the banker rule in the place of the castles of the baron and the earl, and old England has given place to a new England. But it will be this old England of Shakespeare, Warwick and Kenilworth that will live in the hearts of the English people, and will be the object of pilgrimage for Americans abroad.

THE GREATEST OF CITIES.

LONDON, Aug. 11, 1905.

We are "out of season" in London. "Everybody is out of town." I suppose there are only about 7,000,000 people left within the limits of the city as laid out for police purposes. With only 7,000,000 people in this district twenty miles square, one naturally feels lonesome. I suppose it will strike me that way after I get used to it. But if as many of the inhabitants of London as there are people in the State of Kansas should go away, it is probable that I would not notice it at first. It is curious what funny first impressions one gets of things. My first of London was that it looked like a great big ant-heap with the ants excited over something and swarming in every direction. The long processions or streams of people which wind in and out, up and down, make the individual feel mightily insignificant. In comparison my memory of Chicago is that it looks like a deserted country town on Sunday afternoon, and New York a fairly large and busy village.

The streets of London are laid out with no regard for plan or regularity. None of them are straight, and in the course of a few blocks they will be intersected at every angle and possible curve by other streets, which in turn are cut into by more streets. Every now and then there is a "square," or a "circus," either meaning a place where different streets meet head-on and usually stop. A "circus" is a curved square and not a show. A map of London looks like a chicken-yard in which the hens have been very busy scratching. The stranger loses all idea of direction. When the sun shines, which is not often, I have seen it in the north, south, east and west on the same day.

There are no "sky-scrapers." The height of buildings is regulated, and I think the limit is usually six stories. This is a rule which our American cities ought to have but they won't. The climate has the effect of making a new house soon look old, and London is neither bright nor shining in its appearance. But it is the greatest city in the world, and that fact is impressed on the traveler in every direction. There are more Irishmen in London than in Dublin, more Scotchmen than in Edinburgh, more Jews than in Palestine, and in its population are large colonies of people from every country on the earth. Name any article you want or have ever heard of, and it is in London. No business and no trade in any civilized land but has its representative in this city. No great work is done and no enterprise attempted but the fact is known to some one in London. In spite of the great growth and wealth of America, the industry and success of Germany, the thrift and saving of France, the financial center of the world is in London, and other bourses and boards of trade follow the lead or are in fact only branches of the English concern. Every active financial institution in the United States or elsewhere has its London connection through which it draws when it engages in international business or when it goes out of the local sphere of influence. London is the whirlpool to which all the world contributes and from which all the world gets something thrown out.

London is not only the center of business but of literary, artistic and political activity. Especially is this true for Americans. All of our history prior to 1776 is English, and in the annals of the world 1776 is only the day before yesterday. Our writers, as soon as they get their feet on the ground at home, look to London, this clearing-house of literature as of money. London writers, from the time of Shakespeare to Dickens, Thackeray and Kipling, are ours just as much as they are England's. Not an American but recognizes the names of Piccadilly, Hyde Park, Westminster, Temple Bar, Ludgate, the Tower, Tooley street, London Bridge, Charing Cross, Drury Lane, Whitechapel, Billingsgate, and other streets and places in London as familiarly as he does those of places in the nearest city to which he lives. A common history for more than a thousand years, a common literature which cannot be divided, and a common trend of religious and political thought make Great Britain and the United States one people although divided by an ocean and by arbitrary political lines. I think that up to a few years ago there was much prejudice in each country against the other. That has now practically disappeared. Englishmen on the continent and at home have fraternized with us Americans at every opportunity, and no place in London that I have gone but I have been received with unmistakable heartfelt kindness.

After getting comfortably settled the question comes to the tourist, "What first?" And there is so much in London we want to see, that it was a question. I suppose we answered it as every American would, Westminster Abbey. There we spent our first afternoon. I had been afraid of disappointment. I may say I am getting used to finding things which sounded and seemed big when viewed from Kansas, actually getting small and ordinary when right before us. But it was not so with Westminster. The present building was put up by Henry III., in the thirteenth century to take the place of the structure on the same spot erected by the Saxons soon after the year 1000. A few towers and façades were added a century later, but for practically 400 years this grand church has been the national memorial hall of the English people. Although tombs and monuments are on every side, the spacious church is used for service every day, and it is an agreeable memory now that we joined in the afternoon service that day in the hall where kings are crowned and where they are buried, and where men greater than kings have been laid away after their work was done.

The church is very large, the form of a Latin cross, beautifully proportioned, rather gloomily lighted, but impressive in appearance. Of course it was originally Catholic, but being the state church it went Protestant when Henry VIII. turned against the pope, partly because the pope would not recognize his divorce machine. There are not many statues of saints, but up one side and down the other of the double aisles and the little chapels are monuments, usually statues, of the men whose names are England's greatness. I do not mean the kings and queens, for most of them would not by their own merit deserve the honor, but such as these: The Pitts, father and son, who ruled in England a hundred years ago; Fox, Peel, Cobden, statesmen of the world; Beaconsfield and Gladstone, not far apart now; Wilberforce, the philanthropist; Darwin, Newton and Herschel, the scientists; Livingstone, the African explorer, and Gordon, the general; André, who was shot as a spy in America; John and Charles Wesley, the Methodists; Watts, the hymn-writer; Händel, the composer, and Jenny Lind, the sweet singer of a generation ago; Addison, Macaulay, Thackeray, and Dickens; Chaucer, Ben Jonson, and Tennyson, poets laureate; Booth and Garrick, the actors; Spenser and Dryden, and many other poets;— a great aristocracy of learning, and now in the democratic, barrier-razing grave. Then there are nearly all the great English generals of the last four centuries, with heroes whose names are familiar to American school-boys as to English. And in the chapels are the tombs of England's rulers from Edward the Confessor, some great kings and some little kings, some good and some bad, surrounded by the graves of queens and lords and ladies with the familiar names of English nobility. Near the tomb of the great Queen Elizabeth is that of her rival whom she executed, Mary Queen of Scots, the remains of the latter placed there by her son, King James, who by the irony of fate succeeded his mother's enemy. I could go on with the list, but it would be with the reader as with the visitor, only the general effect, with here and there some great name singled out from the rest because of special interest or connection with some great event. And a fact which impressed me was that many men and women were executed by one monarch and their remains brought to Westminster and monuments erected to them by the next.

In Westminster Abbey the kings and queens of England have been crowned since the time of its building. A sovereign may inherit or receive from the representatives of the people the royal power, but he is not fully authorized and empowered to perform the duties of the job, or, to paraphrase a slang expression, his crown is not on straight until he receives it here. There are times when the great church is brilliant with light and resonant with music, when gay uniforms and gowns fill the galleries and aisles, when bells peal merrily and the banners wave from choir and column, concealing for the day the monuments and tombs of the past with their lesson of the end to earthly greatness and the fate of human pomp and grandeur.

The way to see London is from the top of an omnibus. There are no electric or cable lines or any other above-ground means of transportation in London except cabs and 'buses. The underground railroad, called "the tube," is useful for quick traveling from one part of the city to the other, but the 'bus is the ordinary conveyance. It has regular seats on top, and they are always occupied except when the rain comes in torrents. An ordinary drizzle rain does not bother a Londoner. The sight of the long line of omnibuses with people filling the tops of every one of them is in itself a show. I am told there is not an hour in the day when there are not 100,000 people on top of the London 'buses. We have found that we can learn and see more of London sitting next to the driver of a 'bus in an hour than we could in a day with a carriage and guide. The driver is always glad to trade you all the news about the street for a sixpence, and a London 'bus-driver is a man of intelligence and learning; he has to be in order to drive through the jam of traffic and not get lost in the crooked streets. It was like reading a story when we rode down the Strand past St. Paul's and the Bank of England to the Whitechapel, as the driver pointed out the house where Peter the Great lived when in England; William Penn's old home; Somerset House, where queens have lived; the theatre in which the great actors of to-day appear, Covent Garden; Garrick's house; the rooms which Dickens described as David Copperfield's at Miss Trotwood's; the Temple, England's great lawyer factory; the grave of Goldsmith; the inn where Johnson and congenial sports dined and drank; and all kinds of places mentioned or described by Dickens and Thackeray, or connected with the history of England. I am not writing a guidebook, but I can make affidavit that a ride on a London omnibus is the quickest and easiest way I know to fill one's head with a jumble of literature and history, as well as to test the elastic qualities of the neck. If I were to advise a tourist coming to Europe I would not only tell him to read in advance and bring plenty of money, but he should have all the rubber possible between his head and his body.

AT KING EDWARD'S HOUSE.

LONDON, Aug. 14, 1905.

We have spent the day at Windsor Castle, the favorite home of Queen Victoria, and indeed of British monarchs for several centuries. King Edward and Queen Alexandra were not at home. We had not advised them in advance of our intention to visit them, and Edward had gone off to a hot-springs resort to recuperate from the festivities of last week, when he was entertaining the French navy. The queen is visiting her folks in Copenhagen, and none of the royal family were at the depot. However, we went direct to the castle, and, opening it with the usual key (a shilling), we wandered around in the big and beautiful rooms, tramped through the stables and saw the horses, and enjoyed the beautiful view of the valley of the Thames from the terrace on which Queen Elizabeth used to stand and shoot deer which her gamekeeper drove in front of her. King Edward and Queen Alexandra have a right pretty place at Windsor, but it takes a lot of help to keep it up. There are fifty men employed in the stables alone. The queen is a good housekeeper, as can be told from the well-polished floors, the shining brass and the absence of dirt and dust from the walls and furniture. Windsor Castle is about three times as big as the Reformatory. Part of it was built over 800 years ago by William the Conqueror, and it has been added to by nearly every sovereign. It was a favorite place with Henry VIII., and one of his wives, Anne Boleyn, was confined and executed in Windsor. At the time, Henry was over in the next county waiting until Anne was dead so he could marry another, which he did within forty-eight hours. The kings and queens in those days were often tough bats and acted scandalous. They couldn't do it now, at least in England. A few years ago the people of England were worked up over a gambling scandal in which the present king, then Prince of Wales, was implicated. But King Edward has shown himself to be a model monarch, and he and the queen are both popular.

A king does not have an easy job. He has to attend state banquets, preside at the laying of corner-stones, and ride in state on great occasions, always look pleasant when he is in public, and eternally be entertaining somebody from somewhere that he does not care about. This does not sound so bad, but when you read, as you do in the English papers, just what the king does every day and realize what a grind it must be after the novelty is worn off, you begin to feel sorry for Edward. No wonder he has to go to the hot springs for his health. I don't suppose that since he has been king he has had a whole week off, and he is getting old. Kings and queens have to do everything, from marrying to visiting, because it is best for their countries and not because they want to. Even an independent American citizen knows how tiresome it is to do "what is best" rather than what you really like, and poor Edward never gets a rest. Of course, if the king really had power there would be some recompense to a man. But the king of England has little or no power. He is not allowed to have any views on public questions. When the Conservative party is in power it speaks for the king and when the Liberal party is in power it voices the sentiment of the king. This fiction is a part of the British constitution, with the further inconsistent proposition that the king can do no wrong. If the people disapprove of the public policy they blame the dominant ministry, and properly so, for the king has no more to say on political questions in England than a Republican has in Texas. Edward would no more dare to take a decided position or make a stand on a government policy than he would get out in the street with nothing on but his crown. The people run the government in Great Britain nearly as much as they do in the United States, and the monarchical customs and the restrictions and regulations which seem absurd to us would be dumped out in the next session of parliament if the people wished it. But they don't, for they are English and they cling to the old ways. They want the king and nobles and are willing to pay the bills.

But I am getting away from Windsor. It is the biggest and best castle I have seen in Europe. There are towers and turrets and moats enough to remind you that once upon a time a castle was a fort, and there are gardens and terraces and beautiful pictures which show that the kings have spent their money, or the people's money, with good taste. There are several other royal residences in England, but Windsor is conceded to be the best. It is in a beautiful country, and yet it is close to London, so that the king could spend a quiet night and in the morning hop on the train and in thirty minutes be at his office in the city. And the king has a train of special cars nearly as handsome as those of a division superintendent on the Santa Fe.

Our guide pointed out to us a neighboring estate which belonged to William Penn, the first owner of Pennsylvania, long before Quay's time. Penn got the English sovereign to let him have all of Pennsylvania at a nominal rent. He then settled with the Indians on a friendly basis, and the result was his Quaker colony prospered from the start. The contract was that he and his successors and assigns should pay to the king of England so many beaver-skins annually. There have been no payments, so the guide said, since July 4, 1776.

On our way to Windsor we stopped at Stoke Poges, or rather at the church near there, in the graveyard of which Gray wrote his great "Elegy." The little church stands just as it did when Gray was there about 150 years ago. The yew tree, to which he refers, is a veritable monarch, and the woman who shows strangers around said it was 900 years old. In the church are the graves of Gray and his mother, to whom he owed his intelligence and his opportunity. The ivy-covered tower looks down over the crumbling gravestones of those—

ır from the madding crowd's ignoble strife,

'heir sober wishes never learned to stray;

ng the cool, sequestered vale of life

'hey kept the noiseless tenor of their way."

Gray wrote a great poem. He never wrote another in the same class. His reputation is based on the Elegy, and that is enough. It made him famous, and he was offered the position of poet laureate to the king and declined it. A man who will decline a good job like that is almost as rare as a great poet.

We read the poem aloud out in the graveyard underneath the yew tree. It fitted exactly. Gray had touched the springs of sublimity by seeing through nature and telling just what he saw, no more.

In a field near Windsor I saw a mowing-machine, the first I have noticed in Europe. Everywhere else the hay and grass has been cut by hand. I mentioned this fact to the driver, and he was very bitter over the introduction of machinery because it kept men out of an opportunity to work. He told me he was going to America just as soon as he could "raise the funds." The women do not work in the field in England, at least not much. But they are busy in the dairy, at the stores and behind the bar in the saloons. In every way I found England ahead of the continent in its ways of doing things, but there is still enough difference from our ways to make them seem queer. I also have a kick coming on another matter. A great many English people do not speak the English language. They think they do, but they not only drop their h's when they should be on and put them on where they do not belong, but they pronounce the vowels and some of the consonants in a manner that would make a dictionary turn pale. It is often very difficult for me to understand them, and they are all at sea over my Kansas brogue. Of course this does not apply to the educated English people, who only speak differently from us in using a broad and pleasant accent.

Coming down the street on the way home I saw in a grocery-store window these signs: "Breakfast eggs, ten for a shilling;" "Recommended eggs, twelve for a shilling;" "Select eggs, fourteen for a shilling;" "Cooking-eggs, sixteen for a shilling." The frankness of the signs surprised me. I suppose we have the same varieties of eggs in Kansas, but we don't describe them so exactly and they all go at the same price. As eggs are a staple item on the bill of fare, I am wondering to-night whether my landlord buys "breakfast eggs" or "cooking-eggs," or just plain "eggs."

The English money is the hardest to understand in Europe. It is based on the shilling, worth about a quarter in our money. Four farthings make a penny, 12 pennies make a shilling, and 20 shillings make a pound ($4.80). The usual coins are the ½ penny, pronounced "ha-penny," penny, "tuppence," the 3-penny, pronounced "trippence," the sixpence, the shilling, the 10-shilling, the pound, called a sovereign; the 5-shilling piece, called a crown, and the half-crown. You add 8 pence to 10 pence and it doesn't make 18, it makes "one and six." Add one and six to one and eight and it makes three and two—yes, it does! Figuring with English money for an American beginner is like turning handsprings.

The paper currency is issued by the Bank of England, and is made of white-fiber paper. In some way I got possession of a ten-pound note and took it into a bank to have it changed. The cashier had me sign my name on the back. I demurred at first, but as I wanted the change I finally did it, remarking to him that I was pleased to know that the bank considered my indorsement necessary to a bank note of the Bank of England. The cashier did not see the joke, for he took pains to tell me that it was not to make the note better and that a Bank of England note was worth its face in gold anywhere. I have had a hard time with my alleged jokes. I had a letter of introduction to a London banker from a New York banker, and presented it in order to get the opportunity of looking through an English bank. Wanting to be pleasant and friendly, I remarked as he finished reading the letter that I had gotten it so that if I had trouble with the police I might call on him for help. He gravely assured me that he did not think I would have any difficulty with the police. He did not see my little joke. Perhaps he has seen it by this time, for that was two days ago.

THE TOWER AND OTHER THINGS.

LONDON, ENGLAND, Aug. 17, 1905.

After Westminster Abbey I went to looking for the Tower of London. Since I was a boy and read the story of the two little princes who were said to have been murdered in the Tower by order of their royal uncle, I had pictured the Tower as something awful and gloomy. As a matter of fact the Tower is rather imposing in appearance, and with the improvements that have been made in recent years is a fairly decent sort of castle right in the city of London. Built for a fortress by William the Conqueror soon after his capture of England from the Saxons, it was added to and used as a royal residence and state prison, mostly the latter. Kings and queens have been confined within its walls and nobles have been imprisoned by the hundreds, many of them only finding it a step toward execution. It is now a government arsenal, and contains a number of soldiers and a lot of military supplies as well as a historical museum. The Tower consists of a dozen towers inclosed by a wall and moat, and covers thirteen acres. It is really very interesting, and anyone who remembers his English history or who has read English stories of a few centuries ago can feel delightful thrills as he goes up and down the dark corridors and stairways, sees the rooms in which so many of the great men of England, good and bad, spent the time preliminary to their death, or passed years in confinement. Kings of England, Scotland and France, princes, archbishops and ministers of state have carved or scratched their names on the walls and window-frames while sojourning here at the expense of the state. As a usual thing the executions were held outside the walls so that the public could enjoy the amusement, but a few of the noble ladies and some men who were very popular with the people were decapitated in the little square in the middle of the inclosure, and the spot is now marked by an iron tablet. The Tower has not been used as a prison since 1820, and since then it has been cleaned and renovated so that the only evidence of the dark old days is contained in the placards which the government has put up for the benefit of the public. Henry VIII., who was a bad husband but an able monarch, had a fad for the collection of old armor, and a great part of the White Tower, the largest of the towers in the Tower, is taken up by a splendid exhibition of the fighting-clothes and weapons of England and Europe during the Middle Ages. In another tower, Wakefield Tower, is kept a part of the royal regalia, including the crown worn by the king when he is formally inducted into office at Westminster Abbey. This crown contains 2,818 diamonds, 300 pearls and other precious stones "too numerous to mention." The government charges a sixpence to get into this exhibit, which is said by the official guidebook to be worth $15,000,000. You pay another sixpence to see the rest of the buildings, including the old armor, the place where the bones of the little princes are said to have been found, the tower where the Duke of Clarence was drowned in a large cask of wine, and all the other beautiful horrors that go with the Tower. I never fail to appreciate the thrift of these European governments. They always charge admissions to the castles, palaces and public buildings. What a howl there would be in America if the Government should exact a fee of 10 cents to visit the White House, or the State of Kansas should charge admission to the Governor's residence at Topeka.

When we went into the Tower the officers at the gate made everybody leave packages or boxes outside. Mrs. Morgan even had to dispose of her chatelaine bag, and when she wanted to know the reason why, learned that it was to prevent her carrying dynamite into the Tower and blowing it to pieces. The powers of the Old World are always looking for dynamiters.

During our stay in London the French fleet has been visiting the British fleet at Portsmouth, and a large number of the officers and men have been brought to London and entertained. International politics is a subject of general interest in Europe. Emperor William of Germany has most of the rest of Europe so nervous that even the English and French, foes for centuries, are making up to each other. Just as in Germany I found a feeling that eventually Germany would have a war with America and England, I found the same impression here, and as France hates Germany more than it does England, the French, with the same thing in mind, would line up with the Anglo-American combine. The London papers have had numerous articles showing that the combined fleets, armies and financial powers of the three countries and Japan could lick the rest of the earth to a standstill. The most ordinary Englishman is posted on international matters as well as the ordinary American is on local State affairs. To illustrate the public feeling, at a theatre when the ballet-girls were carrying banners of the various nations the climax came with the English representatives and the French representatives clasping hands and the American dancers waving the stars and stripes over them. The audience cheered enthusiastically.

Speaking of theatres reminds me that London has the best in the world. The English people are great play-goers, and the city has such a large population that a play often runs here for a year. Prices are higher for the best seats and cheaper for the cheap seats than in America. A parquet seat is called a "stall," and is usually $2.50. The "pit" is back of the parquet, and is about 50 cents. First balcony is called the dress circle, and is about $2. Second gallery is about 25 or 50 cents. I think the class distinctions account for the great difference in prices. An imposition in London theatres is that a charge of 12 cents is made for a program, filled with advertising, and no better than those given free in America. When the orchestra plays "God Save the King" the audience rises. Americans get up, too, and as the tune is the same as "America" the Yankees I know sing "Sweet Land of Liberty" while the English are saving the king.

I saw the procession of the local officials when the Frenchmen were here. The sheriff of the county rode in a beautiful old-style yellow coach, wore a three-cornered hat and a uniform of 200 years ago, with powdered wig and sword. The lord mayor of London was dressed the same way, with his hair down his back in a queue. If the sheriff of Reno county and the mayor of Hutchinson had any style about them they would not let these English officials outshine them. I am told it costs the mayor about a half-million a year to hold the office, as his principal duty is to entertain the city's guests at his own expense. The lord mayor is more ornamental than useful. The local government is more like our State organization, with one legislative body, consisting of 118 county councillors elected by the boroughs, and another of nineteen aldermen appointed by the council. As London has about five times as many people as Kansas and much harder problems of administration to be solved, the government is a big thing. And London is well governed, better, I think, than American cities. The only thing that would grate on us is the great amount of regulation. You can't build a house or go into business without permission, and then everything must be just so. The English people are law-abiding, more patient with regulations and rules than ours, and public opinion stands for the strict enforcement not only of laws but of what seem like absurd red-tape rules. Hardly any stores are open or business commenced until 9 o'clock. Nearly everybody takes one to two hours for lunch. Stores close at 6 o'clock and dinner is in the evening. Saturday afternoons all business houses are shut up, and there are a great number of holidays. An American gets nervous over the easy-going way of doing business. He is always in trouble because he has forgotten it is Saturday afternoon or a "bank holiday," or because he can't transact important business between 12 and 2 o'clock. In fact, if he wants to, an American can find a lot of things in London to make him miserable and cause him to abuse the country. But if he is patient and learns a little of the English ways he finds that he may live a little slower but he will live just as happily, and probably longer if he does as the English do. The American way of rushing things is well known and generally discountenanced in England. They think we are fools for working so hard, and resent the rather offensive criticisms by the Yankees of their slowness. Perhaps they are right. They tell me that on his first visit an American always tries to reform English business methods. After that first attempt he tackles the easier job of sweeping back the ocean with a broom.

IN RURAL ENGLAND.

LONDON, ENGLAND, August 21, 1905.

We have just finished a trip of a couple of hundred miles through southern England in a motor car. In France and the United States it is an automobile, but in Great Britain it is a motor car. This is a better way to see the country than from a railroad train, and not so good as walking. If you have a motor car or have a friend who has one, that is the best way to travel. If you have none and no prospect, a motor car is a delusion and a mistake. I happened to have a friend with a motor car and am therefore on the side of the motorists.

We left London at 10 o'clock in the morning, and by night had ridden a hundred miles and taken in Hampton Court, Windsor, Reading, Maidenhead, Alton, and Winchester, besides a lot of little places and the country along the way. The English roads are just about perfection. The main roads are made of stone or gravel with clay on top, rolled until they are as smooth as asphalt, and kept free from holes and bumps. Every bridge and culvert is of stone. There is no need to slow up except for people and other vehicles. I doubt if America ever has such roads. Perhaps in a thousand years, when our country is about as old as England, we will have equally as good thoroughfares, but it will be fully a thousand years. These English roads were good stone roads before the days of railways. They were constructed as business and military necessities by the order of the English government. I don't think Kansas farmers will ever build graveled roads on which motorists can make high speed and kill the chickens and dogs that don't get out of the way when the horn blows. However, Kansas farmers could, profitably to themselves, improve their roads so that one horse could haul a wagon-load in place of two horses, and so that the wagon could be hauled in muddy times. Such roads would be good enough for Kansas automobiles, and by that time they will be cheap and every farmer will have one. The Romans who conquered and held possession of England from the time of Julius Cæsar to several centuries later, were great road-builders, and fragments of their old military roads still exist. Good roads are a sign of civilization. Fortunately, they are not the only sign, for if they were, parts of Kansas would be uncivilized. We can beat the Old World on a good many propositions, but when it comes to roads and highways the old country has us skinned a good many blocks.

This is August, but the woods and meadows of England are as green and fresh as with us in May. An English summer as I see it is warm and moist. It is not near so warm as in the Mississippi valley, and the rain comes nearly every day. Rain does not often fall in sheets and inches, but drizzle-drazzles down and soaks in so as to do the most good. The English people don't mind the rain at all. It is this moist climate which covers the walls with ivy and the trees with moss, and keeps the verdure fresh and green until the fall. Harvest is just now being finished. There is no corn in England—although they call barley, wheat and small grain generally, "corn." The principal crop is hay and oats and barley, a little wheat, and vegetables in great quantities. England has 50,000 square miles, so it is over half as large as Kansas, but it has 30,000,000 people, and therefore much of the farming is for market truck. As a matter of fact there is very little actual "rural life." The villages are so close together that it is often hard to tell where one town ends and another begins, and a country road is as nearly well settled as a city suburb in America. Here and there are vast estates, the beautiful show places and curse of England. With millions of people wanting work and thousands of tenant farmers who can get no title to the soil they till, it looks to me like a howling outrage for a lord, a duke or a brewer to fence up several thousand acres as a shooting-place, and remove from production a large per cent. of the land which ought to be doing good and providing some Englishman a chance to make a living and a home. The English people do not seem to mind it at all, and I suppose there is no call for me to get excited, but I can't help it. We have gone by some beautiful parks, with great stately trees, deer grazing in herds and pheasants and quail flying at the side of the road. These belong to somebody who is off for the summer and who got them from his father, who received them from the king, who originally stole them from the actual owners. For quiet beauty the lanes and meadows of England, lined with fine trees and fenced with hedge or stone wall, cannot be beaten. The Arkansas valley is just as beautiful in June, but in August the Kansas sun can be depended on to do business and spoil the freshness of the trees and grass. When the wayside is not inclosed between high hedgerows, the fence is stone, but over the stone grow ivy and moss, out of the cracks come grass and flowers, so the coldness and bleakness of the rock is concealed. Every English farm seems to have a flock of sheep. I always heard the national meat of old England was roast beef, but that is a mistake. It is mutton-chops, and every English family has them at least once a day if it has the price. Along the main roads are little inns every mile or so with the peculiar names and signs that are characteristic. During the day I counted four called "The Red Lion." One was "The Headless Woman," and over the sign-post was the picture of a woman with her head chopped off below the chin. These inns are hotels and public-houses, and generally look interesting and clean. I am told their prices are reasonable to Englishmen, but they charge Americans in an automobile about all the law would allow.

To-day we came from Southampton to Brighton, fifty miles along the southern coast. The beach is fine, and is the summer resort of England. Years ago royalty and nobility made Brighton their favorite sea-shore place, but the great plain people have gotten into the habit of going there in numbers, so the aristocracy has gone farther, to the continent and to Wales. Nearly every one of these old English towns has a cathedral and a Roman wall. The Romans were town-builders as well as road-makers, and they never even camped for the night without fortifying. The cathedrals were mostly built in the Middle Ages, when the church was a wealthy business organization with lands and revenues. They look old and quaint and are generally in good taste. When you read about a cathedral or castle being a thousand years old you may depend on it that if it is still in use it has been "restored." Some of these very old cathedrals remind me of the boy's jackknife. The blades wore out and he got new blades. The handle wore out and he got a new handle. But he still had the old jackknife. A cathedral built in the year 1000 may have new walls, new roof, new interior and new spire, but it is still the old cathedral, "restored."

In a little old English inn on the bank of the river Thames we ate our lunch and watched the endless procession of boats that passes up and down the stream. The ocean reaches up the river as far as London, so that it is really an inlet, with a tide that rises and falls, and a deep channel for ships. Ten miles above London the Thames is about the size of the Little Arkansas, and all the way past Windsor, Henley and Oxford, historic for the boat-races, it is very little wider than Cow creek. By a system of dams and locks the Thames above London is really only a canal. There is a path alongside, and we saw several young men taking their sisters, or somebody's sisters, for a boat-ride, the man walking the bank, pulling the boat with a rope, and the lady sitting in the boat. In some countries I have been in this summer the woman would have been pulling on the rope and the man would have been reared back in the seat, comfortably smoking a long cigar. As a river the Thames above London is not much, but as a pretty winding stream, carrying little steamboats and row-boats, filled with gaily dressed people, it is a success.

The place we stopped for lunch was at Runnymede, just about the greatest spot on earth for English and Americans. It was here in 1215 that King John met the rebellious barons and signed the Magna Charta. Up to that time the king of England had done as he pleased, regardless of law. King John levied taxes so heavily that the people could not stand it, and the big nobles suffered worst of all. So the barons combined, and when the king started out to lick them, his supporters nearly all went over to the rebels. In order to save his neck and his kingdom, John met the barons at Runnymede and signed the agreement which is at the basis of the English and American constitutions. He agreed not to levy any further unusual taxes except by consent of the Great Council of the nobles (origin of the English parliament), nor to deny or sell justice, and confirmed the right of an accused person to a trial by jury.

It did not make any difference if King John repudiated the Magna Charta as soon as he could. The principle was established, and while some English rulers after that tried to evade and escape its provisions, the English people held to it as their rock of refuge. England has no written constitution like ours. The English constitution is a growth of custom, laws, grants and statutes, and the Magna Charta is the basis on which it rests.

When John met the barons at Runnymede the people had no rights that king or baron was bound to respect. But John put a provision in the Magna Charta that the barons must treat their tenants as fairly as the barons wanted to be treated by the king. I suppose John was trying to get even with his powerful nobles by thus recognizing the common people, and deserves no credit for the article. But in a few centuries the development of this idea and the discovery that a musket in the hands of an ordinary man could shoot a hole through a knight, broadened the Magna Charta so that it protects every Englishman.

One of the things that strike Americans as odd is the rule of the road, "turn to the left." This rule is rigidly observed everywhere in England. But when your motor car, running at 30 or 40 miles an hour, meets another coming at a like speed, and your driver turns to the left, the American on the rear seat shuts his eyes so as not to see the collision, while a cold chill travels down his backbone. Of course there is no accident, for the other fellow also turns to the left, but it is hard on the nerves. However, a Kansas man in Europe takes plenty of nerve with him and he is all right so long as his money lasts.

RAILROADS IN EUROPE.

Liverpool, Aug. 24, 1905.

A railroad is a railroad anywhere in the world, only it is sometimes different. Every country has its own peculiarity in railroads as well as in everything else. The first European train we saw was at Queenstown, Ireland, and we laughed. It looked like a toy, small engine, small coaches and strange in appearance. I decided to wait until I had more observations on the subject before putting my ideas into a letter, and since then have gone from one country to another in Europe, traveling first, second and third class, on main lines and branch roads, on through trains and accommodation trains, and gaining all the knowledge possible for an American traveler who gets his information from experience. While each country has its peculiarities, there are certain ways in common.

In the first place the European idea of a passenger car is taken directly from the old stage-coach. It is composed of from three to six compartments, like that many stages fastened together. In each compartment there are two seats running across the car, facing each other, and holding eight or ten passengers. As a rule there is no communication between the compartments. You get in the little room, the door is shut and locked, and there you stay until you get to the next stop, when the door is opened if anyone wants to come in or go out. There is no toilet-room, and no way to go to the smoking compartment unless you are in one, and no way to get out if you are in. I think all third-class cars are of this pattern. On the main lines, on a few trains and in some cars, there is a corridor running along the side, making it possible to go from one compartment to another, and sometimes there is a toilet-room. This pattern of cars is often called "American," and usually there are extra charges. The cars are short and light, with two wheels under each end like wagon-wheels, and not the double trucks of our cars. There is very seldom any ventilation at the top, and as the rule is that the passenger next to the window can regulate its opening, the other passengers can freeze or roast as the case may be. In Germany the cars have appliances for steam heat, but they do not seem to usually have them in England or elsewhere on the continent. Travelers carry rugs, blankets and footstones in cold weather.

And right here let me explain a difference in traveling that accounts for much of the seeming shortcomings of European cars. The people in Europe hardly ever take long journeys. Sleeping-cars are rarities and only carried on a few trains. A European who takes a twenty-mile railroad trip thinks he is a "traveler." They do not have our magnificent distances and long journeys, and therefore do not expect the comforts and luxuries which we consider necessities. Almost the only people who make what are called "long trips" in Europe, that is, ten or twelve hours, are American and English tourists, and they are given a shadow of American comfort on certain first-class trains, for which they pay right well. For example, Mrs. Morgan and I wanted to take the night train from Paris to Marseilles, twelve hours' ride. One train carried a sleeping-car. It left Paris at 9 o'clock at night and reached Marseilles at 9 o'clock the next morning. Only passengers with first-class tickets can ride on it. I bought my first-class tickets (nearly twice the second-class, which is the usual way), and then asked how much the sleeper would be. "Twenty dollars!" In America we would have paid $2.50. And this in a land where we were told everything was cheap! I have often been heard to rail at the high rates charged by Mr. Pullman, but I will be slow to do so again. I lifted up my voice to the French agent on the extortion of charging twenty dollars for one night, and he shrugged his shoulders and said we could go on the day train,— that Frenchmen never used the sleeping-cars, and that if the rich Americans wanted them they could pay the price. We did not buy that sleeping-car, but a few days later, when it became very important to hurry to Rome, we gave up eight dollars for a sleeper from Genoa to the city of the Cæsars. A berth in a European sleeping-car is a little compartment with two beds, one above the other, about the size of pantry shelves. Two people cannot comfortably stand in the compartment, and when one is dressing the other has to stay on his shelf or go out in the corridor which runs along the side. There is no ventilation, and the toilet-room, about as big as a barrel, is for both sexes. As some American said, there is one good thing about a European sleeping-car, and only one: you do not mind having to get off at an early hour.

The railroad language is different in England. When I bought a ticket in London I went to the "booking office," and "booked for Liverpool." There is no conductor, but a "guard," who is conductor, brakeman and porter combined. Freight trains are "goods trains." The engineer is a "driver." Baggage is "luggage." A grip is a "bag," a trunk is a "box," and anything is a "parcel." Nobody calls the stations. When you reach your destination you get off, and if you are a stranger you are always in trouble wondering whether or not you have gone past. I have never learned the theory of their tickets. When I "book" I get a ticket about like ours. Often no one looks at it or takes it up until I leave the station at the end of the trip. We rode one day in Italy nearly all day before anybody looked at our tickets, although usually it is necessary to show them to get on the station platform. It would seem as if such carelessness would be taken advantage of, but it does not seem to be. One reason probably is that in every country it is a crime to ride on a railroad train without a ticket. In America if the conductor catches you riding without a ticket he collects the fare. In Europe he can send you to jail, and I don't doubt but he would. In America it is not considered even bad morals to beat a railroad. In Europe it is a felony.

I had been told that railroad traveling is cheaper in Europe than in America, but it is not. To understand railroad rates you must remember that population is very dense and traffic heavy, much like suburban travel around New York or Chicago. England is not near as large as Kansas, but it has twenty times our population. Practically all of the travel is short-distance. The same conditions prevail on the continent. You can ride third-class, second-class, or first-class. In most countries third-class is a good deal like riding in American box-cars fitted up with seats. That costs about two cents a mile. Second-class means cars such as I have described with upholstered seats, and the price is close to three cents a mile. First-class means plush or leather and a guarantee that your traveling companions will be nobility or Americans or fools. The first-class rate is about four cents. In most European countries no baggage is carried free. You pay extra for fast trains, "corridor trains," and for the use of toilet-rooms. In order to travel in clean company and in ordinary decent style, after you count in your "extras," the railroad fare is just about the same in Europe as in America, and not as cheap as it is on similar trains in the populous sections of our country. In the stations there are separate waiting-rooms and separate lunch-counters for first, second and third-class passengers. The high-class European can eat his lunch with the happy thought that no rude third-class citizen is on the next stool.

But if the European railroads do not do much for the comfort and pleasure of the passengers, they are away ahead of our railroads when it comes to providing for their safety. Accidents are not unknown, but they are rare, especially in comparison with the frightful wrecks which take place in the United States. Nearly every railroad is double-tracked or has three or four tracks. The roadbeds are near to perfection. Bridges are of stone. Rails are not so heavy, but are stronger when the light cars are considered. And every mile of European track is patrolled day and night. They use a half-dozen section-men and track-walkers where we would have one or two, and they pay the half-dozen wages that aggregate about as much as the one or two. In Italy the track-walkers are usually women, and it was a funny sight to see the Dago lady stand with a red flag at "present arms" when the train passed. Most crossings are overhead or under, very rarely on grade. Embankments are built of stone instead of mud, and the roadbeds are constructed for centuries, instead of being just sufficient to "earn the bonds." I was in England when an accident occurred on a railroad, and the next day the matter was brought up in parliament and the government was asked what it was doing to prevent a recurrence of such a thing. Just as the government protects the railroads from beats it regulates their conduct for the safety of the traveler. In some European countries, Germany, Belgium, Switzerland and Italy, the government owns the important railroads, but in all of them it exercises a strong control. If a European railroad would attempt to operate a line like some of the jerkwater branches in Kansas, the directors would be in jail. The result is that many of the conveniences are sacrificed to rigid rules and the lives and limbs of the passengers are not in near as much danger as in the United States, where competition has gone in for comfortable cars and often neglected the track. While the Europeans might copy some of our methods, our railroad officials could get some information in the Old World that would save them lots of wrecks and make their passengers more secure in their life and health while traveling in the palatial cars.

As the European does not travel long distances and has to pay extra for his baggage, he rarely takes anything but hand-luggage. All through Europe we have journeyed for three months, carrying all of our baggage in the car with us. When we reached a station where we were to stop there was always a porter on hand to carry our half-dozen grips and bags, and for five or ten cents put them safely in the carriage that would take us to the hotel to the hotel for a quarter. During the three months I don't think I carried my grip three times. There is always a man standing around ready to do such work so cheaply that nobody thinks of carrying his own grips even across a station platform. If you have a trunk it is put in a box-car on the end of the train, and at your destination you go and get it at once. There are no baggage-checks, and you wonder the trunks do not get lost. But they don't.

The station-master always wears a fine uniform, and in most countries he is a sort of military officer. When the time for departure arrives he rings a bell or blows a whistle. The guards close the car-doors. Then the station-master whistles again and the train starts, the station-master saluting. The engine does not whistle or ring a bell. The conductor does not yell "All aboard!" The station-master is the whole thing. He is an autocrat and has entire control of the train in station.

Trains are rarely late in Europe. The schedule is maintained regardless of connections, and therefore connections are usually made. The railroad rules have the same weight as laws and are observed as such. Railroad employés are polite. When a porter starts down a platform with a barrow of luggage he does not try to run over people, or yell "Get out of the way!" as in America. He goes slowly and calls out "Make way, if you please." Baggagemen do not try to break the trunks, and will answer civilly when you ask questions. Some of these European ways are not so bad.

Summed up, these are my impressions of European railroads: Cars small, uncomfortable, unsanitary; road-bed fine and management good; prices about the same as in America, and chance of getting to your destination much better.

A passenger train with the long line of little light coaches is put over the rails very rapidly in Europe if they wish. Many regular trains make fifty and sixty miles an hour. The ordinary trains which stop frequently and carry the third-class cars principally, are slow. A freight car, called a "goods van," is about the size of a dray. There are not many box-cars, but the goods are packed on the open drays and covered with tarpaulins. The effect is about like a thresher engine pulling a lot of four-wheel wagons and drays. It looks "dinky" and is a cause of merriment for Americans. But the Englishman retorts with some reference to an American railroad wreck and we shut up. I have learned this summer that while the United States is the greatest country on earth, it can still learn lessons from the slow-but-sure-going English, the sturdy Germans and the energetic French. One of these lessons is that fast trains and fine cars ought to be supplemented by solid roadbeds and careful watching.

A New York clothing merchant was showing a customer some suits. The man tried on a coat and vest, and when the merchant turned his back he bolted out of the door. The store-keeper yelled "Stop thief!" and called the police. All joined in the pursuit. The policeman drew his revolver and began to fire at the fugitive. "Shoot him in the pants!" screamed the merchant, "shoot him in the pants: the coat and vest are mine."

So when we begin to fire at the defects of railroading in the various countries I have to beg the shootist to shoot at the pants, the coat and vest and some of the faults are our own.

THE TIME TO QUIT.

Liverpool, England, Aug. 24, 1905.

To-morrow we will finish the job of seeing Europe and sail for home. Just to be sure that we would not miss the boat, we came to Liverpool two days in advance. When an American is on his first long stay in a foreign country and the time grows near when he is to return once more to the land and the people he loves, he knows now that he loved them if never before. Strange scenes are no longer interesting, castles, cathedrals and curious costumes are tiresome, and the only thoughts are of the folks at home. Even a man who is ordinarily cynical and unsentimental finds his heart beating faster as the hours drag slowly by waiting for the time of departure. It would be a great relief if one could walk ahead and be overtaken, but the walking is not good in the Atlantic this season, so we are painfully killing time and going through the motions of sight-seeing while "waiting for the train," or rather for the boat, which happens to be the White Star steamship Republic.

On the way here we spent a day in the town of Oxford. Everybody has read more or less of the great university and its student life. Of course this is vacation-time and the colleges are practically deserted, but we wandered through the buildings and quadrangles and enjoyed the walks and quaint streets. The phrase "classic shades" might well have originated here, for the great trees hundreds of years old, the ivy-covered walls and towers, the inclosed courts and the low-ceiled halls and rooms, all make for a peaceful repose that forms a charming setting for the intellectual life which ordinarily fills the place. There are twenty-one colleges in Oxford, each large in size and impressive in architecture. The style is a quadrangle with a large court or "quad" within, on which the students' rooms face, and usually covered with grass and filled with stately trees. Each college has from 100 to 300 students, and the attendance at the whole university is over 3,000. The "young gentlemen," as Oxford students are called, reside in the college buildings, and each has a bedroom and sitting-room. Meals are either served in the rooms or in the large dining-hall. There are no recitations, and not many lectures. Much of the studying is done with tutors. The intellectual effort of the student is to acquire sufficient knowledge from lectures, tutors and books to pass the examinations. The chief courses of study are the ancient languages, philosophy, mathematics, history, and either theology, law, medicine, or natural science. The range is not near so large as in America and they do not go so much on what we call "practical studies." On the side the men do good work in rowing and cricket, and have all the fun of American students, even if they are supposed to be in and with the gates locked every night at 9 o'clock.

The history of Oxford University dates back to Alfred the Great, but the first authentic accounts of the work are of the twelfth century. All learning was then in the hands of the church, and the first colleges were primarily for the education of priests. Kings, queens and bishops, interested in learning, established first one college and then another, so that by the thirteenth century Oxford ranked with the most important universities in Europe; and then, as education extended to other professions, the colleges widened their courses of study, and the government, while still ecclesiastical in form, became broad and liberal. The colleges have large endowments, plenty of money, and Oxford and Cambridge have educated most of the great men of England in the last 500 years.

Liverpool is a good deal like a big American city. A hundred years ago it was a small town, but by taking the lead in American trade it has become the most important port of Great Britain, and, counting suburbs, has nearly a million population. Its harbor is a deep river, the Mersey, and the banks are solid walls of wharves, docks and wholesale buildings. It is a relief to strike a town where you go to see bridges and factories instead of churches and art galleries. Liverpool is a good place in which to taper off from the old and the curious to the useful and the active. In our hotel here we have electric lights, bathrooms, and an elevator that works. Hotels where you go to bed by candlelight, bathe in a little tub, and walk up four flights of narrow stairs, are interesting and comfortable, but they are better for a three months' stay than for a steady diet. Nearly every guest at this, the biggest hotel in Liverpool, is an American who is getting anxious.

One of the subjects in which I have taken an interest on this trip has been that of the prices of products and labor, comparing them with those at home. I have referred to it frequently, but perhaps a summary will interest the practical American who wants to know "what it costs." In the beginning I want to say I have not yet found a place where "things are cheap," according to the American standard. The ordinary people in Europe get along with things that are cheaper than in America and they do without others, so their cost of living is not so high. The ordinary artisan or mechanic in Europe will live with his family in two or three rooms poorly lighted, ventilated and uninviting. His rent is therefore cheaper than the American mechanic who occupies a little house of his own and has a front yard or a porch. The European mechanic will have meat to eat once a week or once a day, and he and his family will live on what a great many Americans waste—they have to. Therefore he lives more cheaply, and so can an American who puts himself and his family on a diet of soup, potatoes, carrots and turnips. The ordinary European mechanic is assisted in earning a living by his wife and all of his children, while the ordinary American mechanic only expects his wife to do the housework and look after the little ones, and his children are at school until they are nearly ready to work for themselves. The American mechanic will make from $2 to $5 a day, while the European will get from 50 cents to $1.50.

Clothing is cheaper in Europe, and there is none ready made. The family either is wealthy enough to have tailors and dressmakers or makes its own. A tailor will get $1 a day wages, a seamstress 25 cents a day. A "hired girl" gets from a dollar a month to a dollar a week, so if a European has money enough he can have servants—but he doesn't have them, and his wife and children work out. They don't do this spasmodically, or in hard times, but customarily and ordinarily, just as their parents did before them and their children will do after them. Shoes are more expensive in Europe, and not so good. Cotton goods, such as shirts, underwear, etc., are as high or higher. Silk goods, kid gloves and perfumery are much cheaper than in America. The grades of clothing, etc., are different. In Europe the people use ugly and coarse stuff such as our people never use. Groceries are at least as high in Europe as in America. Meat is higher. You can get a "square meal" in the ordinary American small town for a quarter. You can't do it in Europe, but you can get some soup and bread and carrots for ten cents.

The ordinary American workingman figures that by working hard, being economical and having a careful family, he can save enough to be comfortable, educate his children and give them as good a chance as anybody in town. The ordinary European workingman figures that by working hard, being economical and having all his family at work he can escape the poor-house, and his children can have the same chance he has had.

Of course the best prices are paid in the big cities, as in our country, and I will illustrate by some of my own experiences.

In London at one of the finest shops I had my hair cut and shampooed. It cost me 12 cents American money, and in Hutchinson would have cost me 50 cents, in New York at least 65 cents. The barber told me that most English workingmen could not afford to pay 6 cents (or 4 cents in a plain shop) and therefore cut their own hair.

I could have had a tailor make a suit in London for $12 or $15 that would cost me $30 in Hutchinson or $40 in Kansas City. The American tailor can figure out how it is done. But here is a thing that pleased me: The swell shops in London advertise "American tailoring." A European tailor sews beautifully, but he can't fit. The wealthy Englishmen wear clothes that would make a tasteful American have fits. Americans are the best dressed people in the world, and American tailors are considered the best everywhere.

I could live in a hotel cheaper in Europe. The hotel-keeper here pays his men from $6 to $10 a month and his chambermaids and female help from $1 to $3 a month. His meat and groceries cost as much or more than they would in America, but he works them more economically. The main difference is in the "help."

EUROPEAN CLASS DISTINCTION.

"Big fleas have little fleas

Upon their backs to bite 'em,

And the little fleas have other fleas,

And so on, ad infinitum."

In women's wares, silks, embroideries, laces and sewing are cheaper in Europe. Cotton goods, shoes and ordinary clothes are higher.

"Things" are just as high in Europe, people and their labor are cheaper.

England is the natural friend and business competitor of America. There is a marked difference in methods and ways. An Englishman will hold fast to the old and only accept improvements and changes when he is forced to or when he has fully decided they are best. In America we usually think a change is a good thing, and will prefer something new to the old just because it is new, when it may actually not be as good. These are differences in temperament which have their advantages and disadvantages. We could learn from the English and they from us, and a half-way compromise would undoubtedly work best.

The class distinctions are the most unpleasant feature of English life. An American friend was telling me of an incident which illustrates it. He was visiting a wealthy English family, and during his stay had a long and pleasant talk with the gardener. He went away, and afterward came back for another visit. He told his host that he wanted to see the gardener and ask about some shrubs. "Very well," said the host; "but you won't mind if I suggest one thing to you. Don't call the gardener 'Mr. Johnson.' Just call him Johnson. We never speak to a servant as 'Mr.'" That was not snobbery in England. The host was a kind and intelligent Englishman. It is the custom of the country. The custom goes on down the line. The butler would not associate on equal terms with the footman or the footman with the porter. And the host of my friend would take off his hat to the good-for-nothing son of an earl, who in turn would not presume to approach a prince unless requested. It reminds me of the poem:

"Big fleas have little fleas

Upon their backs to bite 'em,

And the little fleas have other fleas,

And so on, ad infinitum."

It is funny, but it is sickening to an American who knows that in his country the son of the gardener may be President and the son of the President may be a gardener and either of them may be a gentleman if he is honest and straight and decent.

A thought which comes to me very strongly is that a little visiting in other countries not only makes a man a better American, but it gives him the knowledge that there are other bright, smart and able people besides those in the United States. The competition in this world is keen, and every country has its advantages and its disadvantages, its weak points and its strong points. There is no profit in belittling the other fellow. If I have dwelt most upon the differences between America and England, it is because they are the interesting things. There is no interest in what is the same at home and here. The English are a great people. A little country not as big as Kansas really dominates the financial and political world. Out of the false notions of medieval times they have built up constitutional liberty and have conferred its blessings upon others. England is the greatest commercial power on earth, and it is so because of Englishmen and not because of natural advantages or favored position. It is old and interesting, wealthy and powerful. It is good to look upon and pleasant to visit. But as for me, I am with the Kansan who wrote:

been off on a journey—just got home to-day.

aveled north, and south, and east, and every other way.

een a heap of country, and cities on the boom,

want to be in Kansas, where the sunflowers bloom."